To Catch the Wind

To Catch the Wind

Eddie Cairns & Dan Wooding

To Catch the Wind
Published by Mission Outreach NZ
with Castle Publishing Ltd
New Zealand

First published 1992
in the United States of America by:
D/W Publishing Co.
311-C No. Tustin Ave.
Orange, CA 92667

Revised and updated 2022

© 2022 Mission Outreach NZ Trust Board

Original copyright 1992 by Eddie Cairns & Dan Wooding
transferred to Neil & Wendy Mossop
and Mission Outreach NZ Trust Board in 2020.

ISBN 978-0-473-65275-3 (Softcover)
ISBN 978-0-473-65276-0 (ePUB)
ISBN 978-0-473-65277-7 (Kindle)

Production & Typesetting:
Andrew Killick
Castle Publishing Services
www.castlepublishing.co.nz

Cover Design:
Paul Smith

All scripture is from
The Holy Bible, King James Version

ALL RIGHTS RESERVED

No part of this publication may be reproduced,
stored in a retrieval system, or transmitted
in any form or by any means, electronic, mechanical,
photocopying, recording or otherwise,
without prior written permission from the publisher.

Forewords

Rick Warren once said, 'A missionary is not one who crosses the seas, but one who sees the Cross.'

You are about to read a story that is so impressive, you'll find it extraordinary. Every word of it is true. When a man and his family surrender themselves in obedience to the Great Commission of Jesus Christ, the results can surprise you. Truth can be more astonishing than fiction.

There were times when I travelled the road with Eddie. Now you can travel with him too, as you read these pages. You will experience the tensions and conflicts, the love and loyalties that made Eddie 'one who sees the Cross.' You'll meet others who saw it too; people who sacrificed their all to make a difference in our world.

A farmer, a butcher, a mortician, a husband, a father, a grandfather, a brother, a preacher, a visionary and a missionary – how do you put all of these into one man? Eddie's story shows it can be done.

And it does more ... *To Catch the Wind* proves that a single life can make a difference. How? Eddie recognised the spiritual nature of the revolution to which God calls us. When you recognise it too, you will know that you can help the cause of Christ anywhere. You can help it to the degree you are willing to care, to learn, to sacrifice, to suffer, to pray, to support, to give and to go. From then on, *you* will see the Cross.

The world has staged many revolutions, but Eddie went where that spiritual revolution needed him most. He did so at home in

New Zealand, on the shores of China, in Kim Il-sung's North Korea, among the tribes of Burma and in Gorbachev's Moscow.

We need more Eddies, more people who see the Cross. We need more who feel the need, who count the cost, who know that God is sending them and who are obedient to His command. We need more people who love Him so much that they, like Eddie, are available to take the Good News across the street, across the border and across the sea.

To Catch the Wind is a powerful and real story. You will meet the Saviour in this book. You will see the Cross.

The cause of Christ has been called a noble cause, and we've had a chance to see how noble a dedication Eddie truly had. While busy for the Lord in Bangkok, Thailand, Eddie suffered a stroke that partially paralysed one side of his body. I rang Bangkok from Seattle, Washington. I told Eddie he needed to rest.

'That's impossible! I've got to preach next Sunday!' he replied in words slurred by the damage from the stroke.

'You can't do that, you're sick!' I protested.

'But if I don't, who will? Tell me, why aren't there more who will get on with the job for Jesus?' Eddie moaned.

The cry of his heart stayed with me. Each of us needs to be 'one who sees the Cross.' Only then will the world be won for Christ.

Brother David

Brother David (**Doug Sutphen**)*, author of* God's Smuggler to China *and* Walking the Hard Road*, was the founding President and CEO of East Gates Ministries based in the USA. He served with a team of Chinese believers and Ned Graham, youngest son of Dr and Mrs Billy Graham. We thank and honour this man of God for his faith in the Lord and commitment to his call to the body of Christ and believers in China. Brother David crossed his final border on 8 May 2007.*

To Catch the Wind is an inspiring and gripping account of one couple's courageous obedience to follow the leading of the Holy Spirit.

With candid transparency, the reader is pulled into Eddie's dramatic story of his early life that was headed for destruction and the contrasting transformation that happened to him after he gave His heart to the Lord.

'Thrust me out Lord,' became Eddie's heart cry to the great needs of the 'harvest field' he saw around him in New Zealand and within the suffering church worldwide. Three basic premises formed the foundation of what has become a dynamic organisation called Mission Outreach founded by Eddie and Betty… give generously as led of the Spirit, pray believing prayers as led by the Spirit, and simply 'Go' as led by the power of the Holy Spirit.

Since the time of its inception, Mission Outreach has passionately led the way for others to believe God to do the impossible – from Operation Pearl – a million Bibles miraculously into China, to training thousands of pastors throughout Asia who have planted countless numbers of churches.

We've experienced first hand the power and generosity of Eddie's 'prayer room' over our ministry with far-reaching results.

It will be hard to put this book down once you start reading… it will convict you, it will challenge you and if you are willing, God will use it to transform your life as you too *Catch the Wind* of the Holy Spirit.

David and Linda Cowie
Founders – Marine Reach
www.marinereach.com

Whenever you met Eddie, he wanted you to meet his Lord and Saviour, Jesus. If you already knew Jesus, he would pray for you and the Lord would often give him a word and vision for you. He loved talking about Jesus.

Eddie was always passionate about what the Lord was doing in New Zealand and in the access-restricted nations of Asia. His plea for these restricted nations was, 'They need Bibles. We have to take Bibles to our brothers and sisters who are suffering for Christ.' He told the Lord, *'Here I am Lord, send me'* (Isaiah 6:8).

During his ministry years, the Lord sent Eddie to over 50 nations sharing the Gospel and taking Bibles. His deep faith and willingness to obey the call of the Lord to go into all the world and preach the gospel was an inspiration to many. In 1975 Eddie and Betty, along with other friends, started Mission Outreach and many people from New Zealand, Australia and USA became involved in teaching and taking Bibles into access-restricted Nations. Over 47 years later Mission Outreach is still involved in these nations and many more.

Eddie was a good friend, brother and mentor in the Lord to me for over 30 years. I loved the heart of this incredible man; his passion for the Lord and people never ceased.

Eddie crossed his final border to be with his blessed Saviour on 2 December 2021. At the time of writing this, Betty was in a retirement village in Mount Maunganui. They were a great encouragement to me and the Board of Mission Outreach who are continuing the work he started.

As you read this amazing true story and faith-filled journey, my prayer is that it will inspire and encourage you to be bold to step out in God so you too may *Catch the Wind* of His Spirit as Eddie Cairns did.

Neil Mossop
Director
Mission Outreach NZ Trust Board

Contents

1. A Mountain of Bread — 11
2. Like Father, Like Son — 21
3. 'You Have to be Born Again' — 29
4. For Better, For Worse — 41
5. Girls' Town — 51
6. Thrust Me Out, Lord — 63
7. Tortured for His Faith — 73
8. The Voice of God — 81
9. A Giant Prison Camp — 89
10. War Manoeuvres in Albania — 105
11. Danger in the Land of the 'Great Leader' — 115
12. The Pearl of Great Price — 131
13. In the Air to Mandalay — 147
14. Revelations on the Ho Chi Minh Trail — 157
15. The Roof of the World — 171
16. Miracles in Moscow and Cold Water in Havana — 187
17. To Catch the Wind — 199
18. A Tribute to Eddie Cairns — 215

Epilogue: Eddie's Legacy Continues… — 221
About the Authors — 245

Chapter One

A Mountain of Bread

'There she is, Eddie. Brand spanking new. The grand ship, *Michael*.' Bruce's voice carried with it an air of excitement. As we approached the 128-ton ocean-going tug, I could hardly hold back my excitement. This ship had recently been purchased in Singapore for a task that could change church history in the world's most populous nation, China.

'She's exactly like I saw in the vision,' I exclaimed. At her stern was the *Gabriella,* a huge barge attached by a tow rope. What a sight. There were one million Bibles, 232 tons of them, wrapped in green plastic covers, packed tightly together on *Gabriella*'s deck.

We were bobbing and rolling in the brown waters of Hong Kong harbour, at the mouth of the mighty but muddy Pearl River, on the southeast coast of China. Our little *wallah wallah* seemed insignificant among the huge freighters that were docked all around us. The proud owner of our little vessel assured us that he knew the way to the tug-boat, so we entrusted ourselves to him.

I clapped my hands over my ears as a jumbo jet roared overhead to land on a runway at Kai Tak International Airport. The huge 747 was a strange contrast to the small timeless fishing sampans that sailed majestically by, sculled with great skill by Chinese girls. Small lighters adorned in blue, yellow, and green were hurrying to unload the freight ships anchored in the channel, while other *wallah wallahs* took their passengers to various other destinations.

Hong Kong Harbour was a hive of activity that afternoon in June, 1981. To us it seemed like total confusion, but everyone else appeared to know what they were doing.

As I fixed my eyes on the *Michael* again, excitement rose within me. I was to become part of her crew on a mission like no other. My boating experience had been limited to brief excursions on a seventeen-foot sailing boat with the Boy Scouts in New Zealand. Now, here I was, about to become a crew member of a real ocean-going vessel.

Ours was an international team of men. We all had one heart, and that was to get the Word of God to the people of China. There were few in the world, at that time, who knew of our intentions. The daring plan had been given the code name, Project Pearl, and what a pearl it was meant to be. We were going to deliver one million Bibles to China in one night.

This request had come from Chinese church leaders to Brother David, a burly ex-Marine from the United States who was then the Asia director of Open Doors with Brother Andrew, a mission started by the Dutch-born author of the best-selling book, *God's Smuggler*. The church leaders had requested that the Bibles be in the new simplified script of China, the Union Version. With that we had obliged. Now it was a matter of making the daring delivery!

Brother David's eyes began to shine as he spoke to the group of Kiwi (New Zealand) Christians sitting around him in an office some months earlier. 'Brothers,' he began, 'as you know, we have received a request for one million Bibles for China. That's where you come in. We need your help.'

This extraordinary man of faith had become one of my closest friends. He had first arrived at my home in Tauranga, located in the beautiful Bay of Plenty, in 1976 with another American, Johnny Mitchell. Our hearts were immediately knit together as we shared the same vision, providing the Word of God to people locked behind man-made doors; iron, bamboo, and sugar-cane curtains. We had prayed and wept together for China. And we continue to encourage one another in our ministries.

Brother David told us in that Auckland meeting that he had already been able to lay the keel for a barge that was being built in the Philippines. 'The Bibles will soon be printed, but we need a good tug-boat,' he said. 'We have made inquiries around the world, but, so far, nothing suitable has been found.'

John, the chairman of Open Doors New Zealand, chipped in. 'This would be a good time to pray, and seek the Lord concerning this great endeavour.' There was a time of prayer, then Maurice, another member of the Open Doors New Zealand board, broke in, 'I believe God is telling me that this boat is in Singapore.'

Brother David was confused. 'But I'm not going through Singapore,' he said. 'I leave from here to Australia and then to the Philippines.'

As we continued in prayer, a vision appeared before me. In it I saw a large tug-boat in its cradle on the waterfront behind cream-coloured sheds. The area was enclosed by high wire-netting, at the left of the entrance stood some trees.

While I related to the group what I had just seen, a young lady from the office entered the room and said to Brother David, 'Qantas, the Australian airline, has a strike on its hands, so I've re-routed you through Singapore.'

We looked at each other and smiled knowingly. This was indeed the hand of the Lord.

Two days after the meeting, Brother David called me at my home. 'Hello, brother!' blasted the husky voice at the other end of the line. I immediately recognised it as the voice of my burly American friend.

'I found it,' he said.

'Found what?' I asked, puzzled. 'It was just like you said,' he pressed on, hardly able to suppress the joy in his voice. 'I got off the plane in Singapore, took a taxi and asked the driver to take me to the shipyards. I told him I was looking for a tug-boat.

'We approached the waterfront. I saw the trees, the cream buildings and the wire-netting, just like you described, and said to Judy (his wife), 'This is it!'

'I stopped the driver, got out of the taxi and went around the building. There it was, the tug-boat in its cradle.

'I've made negotiations to buy it. Keep praying brother. We'll need another miracle to pay for it.' He told me that he had already been able to raise US $100,000, then added, 'But we only have ten days to come up with the balance. I'm flying to Japan in the morning to talk with my colleagues, then on to the States.'

'The Lord is able, brother,' I reassured him. 'We will continue to pray.'

The phone rang again the following week. It was Brother David, calling from America this time. 'We've taken another great victory,' he said excitedly. 'We have the money for the tug-boat.'

David told me he had been to see Pastor Chuck Smith, senior pastor of Calvary Chapel of Costa Mesa, in Orange County, California.

'After hearing of the need, he gave me a check for $380,000,' David said. 'It's a real miracle.'

When I hung up the phone, I said to my wife, Betty, who had been hovering nearby, 'Let's believe God for me to be in on the Bible delivery.'

Brother David was soon back in New Zealand. When we met and clasped each other's hands with exuberance, it was as if we had never been apart. We walked the empty streets of Auckland in the early hours of the morning while I shared my heart's desire with

A Mountain of Bread

him. Foremost on my mind was Project Pearl, and I told him, 'I would like to be in on the delivery of the million Bibles, brother.'

His eyes clouded. 'Brother Eddie,' he said, 'it could cost you your life.'

'I don't know if anyone is ever really ready to die. Are they?' I responded. 'But I don't think I've ever been more ready than I am now.'

Brother David then asked, 'What will Betty say?'

'I know she wouldn't stop me,' I replied confidently. 'She's already aware of my desire to go.'

My American friend explained that a full crew had already been recruited. 'But,' he promised, 'if anyone pulls out, you'll be the first one in.'

I told Brother David that I would prepare for the scheduled date of delivery, April 18, 1981; I planned, somehow, to go along on that Easter morning mission – Resurrection Day!

Betty and I prayed that things would work out so that I could be there. I made arrangements to transfer everything to her in case I never returned from the dangerous mission.

As the delivery time drew near, Brother David still hadn't been back in contact with me.

'Why hasn't he called me?' I asked Betty anxiously.

'Maybe they don't need you,' she said.

'But,' I protested, 'I'm sure the Lord means for me to be there. I've prayed about this a great deal.'

Easter morning came, and I was still in New Zealand. 'I can't believe that I'm still here,' I told my wife. 'I almost feel that God has died – abandoned me. I'm going downstairs to pray in the office.'

After a few minutes, I ran back up the stairs. 'Honey, I'll be on the ship,' I said excitedly.

'But it's too late,' she protested.

'No, the Lord has shown me that the 'bread' was not delivered.'

'What did you see?' she asked.

'I saw a plate in China. It had no bread on it,' I told her with confidence.

That same Easter morning, I phoned Roly, the director of Open Doors New Zealand who had been at our meeting with Brother David, and told him what the Lord had shown me.

'That can't be right,' he said. 'The last message that we received said that everything was ready to go.'

Undeterred, I waited. Two weeks went by. I waited some more, sure that what I had seen was accurate. Then, Roly phoned me back. He sounded surprised. 'You were right, Eddie,' he declared. 'The Bibles didn't go in, and I have just had a call from Hong Kong asking for you and two other New Zealanders to come immediately. Mark, my son, can be one. Do you know of another?'

'Yes,' I said, 'I'll ask Ivan.'

In a few days we were all safely in Hong Kong where we discovered why the original delivery had been cancelled. Someone had had a vision of twenty bodies floating face down in the water off the coast of China, so they'd cancelled the trip.

Was this just so that I could be here? I wondered.

Our little *wallah wallah* finally nudged up to the stern of the *Michael* as members of the crew reached out to help us aboard. Three of us, Ivan, Mark, and I, were exhausted from our flight out of New Zealand, and it felt so good to have finally reached our destination. The tiny 'ferry' disappeared and we were happy to be aboard the magnificent *Michael*. We unloaded our luggage and surveyed the new surroundings that would serve as home for the time being. After unpacking, I went up on deck with my fellow Kiwis. We watched with fascination as ferry boats moved flawlessly between

A Mountain of Bread

outlying islands, carrying shift workers back and forth. Crowding the water fronts were ancient junks, bringing food to the Crown colony from mainland China.

'The captain's looking for you,' said George, a friendly young fellow, and part of our crew.

'Where is he?' I asked.

'Oh, here he is now.'

I turned to see a well-built man sporting a grey-streaked beard approaching.

'Hi, I'm Captain Karl,' he said, thrusting his hand toward me. 'Welcome aboard!'

'Things are pretty routine for the moment,' he said. 'We've been stuck here for nearly two months. As for your duties, I have a job for you and Ivan that our young men hate – cleaning out the toilets. Once you've done that, maybe you could give our chef a hand in the kitchen.'

I told this experienced 'sea dog' that we were willing to do anything he wanted us to do. Mark, our other New Zealand companion, was soon found helping the other men with their routine, on-board duties. By the way the captain spoke, I guessed that these longshoreman-type chores weren't the most important things on his agenda. It wasn't long before he revealed his heart.

'You'll find you have plenty of time on your hands,' he said. 'I would like you to take as much time as possible to pray. We really need some answers around here.'

It seemed the whole project was in danger of stagnation, and no one seemed able to 'free' it up.

I took Captain Karl's request very seriously. 'Ivan,' I said, 'let's go across to the barge right now and sit on the mountain of 'bread' and pray.'

We scrambled between the tug-boat and the barge. Beneath us were 232 one-ton packages of Chinese Bibles sealed in green plastic covers and tied with ropes. The Bibles had been printed in Nashville, Tennessee, by the Thomas Nelson Company, then shipped to San Francisco. From there, they went by container to Hong Kong where they were loaded onto the *Gabriella.*

As we prayed, I felt God giving me a divine revelation that the Bibles we were sitting on were entombed as Jesus had been in the tomb in Jerusalem. Not until they were released into the hands of the people of China, would they go forth in resurrection power.

The Lord was revealing to me by his Holy Spirit that as Satan had descended for the battle at Calvary, so He had come down to fight with us in this project. The revelations made me acutely aware of the seriousness of this battle.

The summer sun was beating down on us, so Ivan suggested that we go back into the *Michael's* look-out. We climbed the ladder and sat down to pray. Before we started praying, I gazed out across the harbour. In the distance rose row upon row of magnificent, modern skyscrapers clinging to the sides of the mountains on Hong Kong Island, right to the peak. They disappeared into fluffy cotton clouds.

'You know, Ivan,' I told my friend, 'I read somewhere that Hong Kong in Cantonese means 'fragrant harbour', a name that some think came from the incense-making factories that once dotted the island. Another theory is that the name came from the for-trade cultivation of scented pink *bauhinias* which is now the national flower.'

As we waited upon the Lord, I closed my eyes and 'saw' something that troubled me. Three men were standing in single file, facing the same direction. Their right arms were bent at the elbows, and as those behind clasped the right forearms of the men in front of them, a serpent wound itself tightly around them, binding all of their arms together in an unmovable position.

I recognised that these were leaders, and that their right arms of strength had been bound. As I studied the vision, I began to understand why the ship had been loaded in the harbour, but not able to move in all of this time.

As Ivan and I walked past the Captain's cabin, Karl appeared in the door. Reluctant to speak of what I had 'seen', I said, 'How are things going, Karl?'

'Not very good,' he said. 'If we don't move soon, I'm heading home. We're coming into typhoon season and it's getting dangerous for us to remain here.'

This released me to tell him what I had 'seen'. I related the vision to him, then asked, 'Who are the three leaders of this operation? It seems they cannot move.'

He listened without comment, then suddenly climbed over the side of the boat and into a rubber Zodiac, started the engine and headed for Kowloon which is part of what is called Hong Kong. It is a beautiful cluster of 236 islands, and a peninsula from which rise twenty mountain peaks more than 1,000 feet tall, two of them towering 2,000 feet.

Returning later in the afternoon, he told me that he had gone to spend time with Brother David who was on shore at that time.

'I want you to spend as much time in prayer as you possibly can,' he said urgently. 'We sure need divine intervention as soon as possible if we're going to accomplish this mission.'

A spirit of despondency hung heavily on the crew. Many of them had been sitting on the ship for a number of weeks and were weary of the routine. They were stuck in the middle of the harbour and apparently were not going to go anywhere.

My optimism seemed to jar some of them. A crewman named Peter came up to me and said, 'What do you know about all the pressures we've been under? We're not going to deliver these Bibles. We're going to store them in a shed!'

His statement shocked me, but as the days passed, I realised that several of the men on board shared the same expectation. I did come to understand their frustrations. Many of them had been away from wives and families for a long period of time and there was no indication that the delivery would ever take place.

Our mountain of 'bread' was still in the tomb and some wondered if it ever would be resurrected!

CHAPTER TWO

Like Father, Like Son

The year was 1935 and Adolf Hitler and his storm-troopers were beginning to goose-step their way across the fractured face of the Third Reich.

As storm clouds of war gathered in Germany, people in our motherland of Great Britain were not even thinking of the terrible possibility that the war could come to them as they began celebrating the Royal Silver Jubilee of King George V.

As this was occurring in Europe another historic event was about to take place 10,000 miles away in the South Pacific nation of New Zealand, or as the Polynesian voyagers who came across our country 600 years earlier called it, Aotearoa, meaning 'Land of the Long White Cloud.'

The date was May 28, 1935, and a baby was being turned upside down for a hard slap on the bottom. A high-pitched squeal was the first sound he ever uttered. The scene was the maternity annex of the Whakatane Hospital in the Bay of Plenty, a beautiful resort and farming area of our small island country which makes a slender, slanted outline close to the bottom of the world, astride a line midway between the Equator and the South Pole. Lottie Cairns, a nineteen-year-old girl, had just given birth to her first child – Edward Roy, or Eddie, as I was soon to be called.

The nation 'down under' and Mr and Mrs Cairns were just emerging from a devastating depression. To add to the hardship, I arrived on the scene – another mouth to feed. My father was a hard-working man who struggled along with the rest of our nation, for bare survival. My earliest memories were of living on a farm in the Te Puke area of the North Island, forty miles from where I had been born.

Dad was employed as a dairy farm labourer. When the Second World War broke out, my father volunteered for military service overseas, but because of the shortage of farm labourers in New Zealand at the time, his employer had applied for him to be allowed to stay behind. The application was granted and my father was rather disappointed because two of his brothers were already serving the King in Europe.

The authorities in New Zealand had ruled that it was necessary to keep our farms functioning to help meet the need for food in Great Britain, which was being bombed nightly by Hitler's air force as the fliers of the Royal Air Force fought a desperate rear-guard action to keep them at bay.

'Stop the noise,' said my father as he tuned in Radio New Zealand to garner the latest war news. This nightly ritual had become a sacred time in our home. The African campaign was not going well for our troops, and with one of my uncles over there fighting Rommell, my father became deeply concerned for his safety.

My grandmother often stayed with us. Grandfather had been killed in a mining accident in Australia when Dad was a small boy, and the family had moved to New Zealand. My grandmother eventually married again.

Sometimes as a special treat, I was allowed to stay at her home. She lived in Thames, eighty miles away, with her eldest daughter, my father's sister. Her second husband had also died. Grandma had a tiny apartment upstairs in this rather large house. Whenever I was there, I slept by grandmother's side in her double bed.

Often, I would still be awake when she came to bed. She would kneel down to pray and I would try to keep awake until she had finished. All too soon, however, my lids would become heavy and I would drift off. I was never sure how long Grandma prayed, but when I woke up in the morning, she was again on her knees. I would look to see if she had slept in the bed at all. Sometimes there was no evidence that she had. *Has she been praying all night?'* I would ask myself. I never did find the answer to this puzzling riddle.

My grandmother was a strong lady who belonged to the local Salvation Army. I would park myself in front of her old rocking chair and she would pick up her Bible and read stories to me out of the Old Testament. I particularly liked hearing about David, and I longed to be as strong as Samson.

Although Grandma was a committed Christian, her children were far from God. The downstairs of the house had been turned into a gambling den where my auntie Ella ran an illegal bookmaking operation. People from all over the area would phone in their horse-racing bets. Others would bring them to the front door.

'I want you to keep your eye on the gate and run in and tell me if you see a policeman approaching,' my auntie would instruct me. I was scared of this dangerous assignment, and I wondered anxiously if people who came through the gate were actually undercover cops. By 2 p.m., once the off-course betting had closed, I would receive my reward (one shilling and six pence) to go and see an afternoon movie in the town's only cinema. I enjoyed the make-believe world of the movies.

At night, the lounge was turned into a mecca for card gamblers. I would peek in and see neighbours with cigarettes drooping from their mouths, and the tables loaded with bottles of beer. Cigarette smoke hung heavily over the tables like a thick, blue haze and caused me to cough loudly. The air smelled old and stale.

Whenever grandma caught me spying, she would roughly pull me away. 'It's not good for you to watch that filth young man. It's time you were in bed.'

Although my dad was a hard-working man, he drank heavily and was a very self-indulgent man. His expensive habits cost us dearly, making us poor even in terms of New Zealand's modest standard of living.

School was never a pleasure for me, especially because of the old, worn-out clothing I often had to wear.

'What are you looking at?' I said defensively one day as a young boy's eyes bore in on the seat of my pants.

'You've got a patch on your trousers and it's coming adrift,' smirked Peter Smith who was always well dressed.

'Mind your own business, or I'll clout ya!' I threatened him as tears of humiliation stung my eyes. I would often walk with my rear end toward a wall so that the girls at school would not notice my problem. I'd ask mother for new trousers, but she'd always say, 'Dear, we cannot afford them. They're clean and they're paid for. Give them to me and I'll mend them for you.'

I know now that my mother shared some of my pain, but she also tried to put a positive shine on our various problems. She had three sons: myself, Arthur and Peter and would often say: 'If you look for the best in people, you'll always be happy yourself.'

I admired her optimism in the face of what should have been crushing difficulties. There was only one thing that was able to destroy her equilibrium, and I discovered what it was one day when I heard her cry out, 'The cows are trampling all over my garden!'

I flew into action to remove the offending creatures while mother tearfully surveyed the damage. Gardening was her only recreation and I did what I could to comfort her, and set things back in order. By now, she had two more children, Ella and Warren. Life for her was busy and these were difficult years in my life. There was little time for fun. My day usually began in the same way. Father's heavy footsteps became like an alarm clock. When it was 3:45 a.m. he would poke his head through the darkened doorway and shout,

'Come on, boy.' I knew exactly what he meant. I was expected to jump out of bed, get dressed, and head straight for the cowshed.

On two occasions, however, I committed the unpardonable sin of going back to sleep, only to be roughly awakened by my angry father. Without even being allowed to stretch or yawn, I was forced to jump out of bed while he began lashing my tender backside with his leather belt.

As I scrambled toward the cowshed, he would chase me, swinging his belt as I whooped and danced to get out of its way. My small face would pucker woefully, but he paid little heed to the tears that streamed down it. By the time I would emerge from my early-morning chores in the shed, the world was no longer grey and still but yellow with dawn, and noisy with bird song and the scurrying of rabbits. I was still feeling grey, however.

My secondary education suffered considerably because of my early morning 'job'. To be honest, I detested every aspect of school – the regimentation, the monotony and the bully-like brutality of some of the teachers.

'Cairns, have you gone to sleep again?' shouted one of them. He grabbed my hair as if I were a barbarian who should be taught how to behave in a civilised society.

'I'm sorry sir,' I would say trying to hold back my tears. Getting so little sleep at home meant that I had to get more whenever possible. School was as good a place as any.

My father and this teacher were to have several violent disagreements over my working in the cowshed before school. On one occasion, the teacher kept me in all afternoon which meant I didn't arrive home on time for the evening milking session.

The following day, my father went to the school and brutally told the teacher what he thought of him, 'Don't you ever keep my son in school again or you'll get what for,' he warned.

The teacher heeded the warning and never again kept me late, but he made it uncomfortable for me during the rest of my high school years with a barrage of sarcastic comments in front of the other pupils.

'Hurry up, boy, we need to get down to the market garden before it gets away from us.' My father's tone was urgent. He had leased some ground about half a mile from our home and was growing vegetables for sale.

'But I'm supposed to be playing rugby today,' I protested.

'The garden is more important than rugby, boy. Call them and tell them you can't come.'

Like any red-blooded Kiwi, I loved rugby. It was every boy's ambition to represent New Zealand overseas as a member of the 'All Blacks,' our national rugby team named for their black jerseys. I so enjoyed the game and yet my local team could not rely on me to be there on the day of a game. I was angry that Arthur, my younger brother by two years who represented the Thames Valley Rugby Football District Team, was always able to go.

I don't know why I always have to miss out, I thought. *Other kids are allowed. Why should I have to work? I go to practice at night and then I'm not allowed to play.* I felt depressed and inadequate and began to give myself up to daydreams.

Tears of frustration and anger burned my eyes as I toiled in Dad's garden instead of playing my beloved game. *Why do we need this stupid garden anyway?* I thought. *I don't get anything from it!* As I hoed the ground around the cabbages and picked the weeds, I knew all that happened was that my father would use the money to drink even more. My work that day was more irksome than ever.

There must be more to life than this, was a constant thought. I would shiver, feeling as though the very ground under my feet was no longer solid.

All I seemed to do was work, go to school to be picked on by the teachers, and then work some more. My reward for all of this was to bear the public shame of my father's drunkenness, and never to find his approval for anything I did.

Arthur, on the other hand, always seemed to gain Dad's favour. As Arthur became more successful as a sportsman, Dad grew more and more proud of him. I was just a failure in his eyes!

When I reached the age of fourteen, I began to go down the same tracks as my father. For years he had brewed his own beer and had stored it in our wash house. During his drunken stupor, I would help myself to three or four bottles of his potent brew. Then under cover of darkness, I would carry the bottles to a secret hiding place behind a bush near the side of the road. There, my friends and I would consume it.

'Are you free tonight, Bruce?' I asked my young neighbour.

'Same place, same time,' he smiled knowingly.

My drinking habit was increasing as I began going to parties with guys who were usually much older than I.

I was drifting into an inescapable mess. What I hated in my father, I found myself now doing. Drinking transported me temporarily from the stark reality of my life, but there was a down side. When I was sober, fear and anger were still my constant companions.

What does the future hold for me? I wondered almost daily. *Is there any escape from this poverty mentality?*

'Sing us a song, Eddie,' the master of ceremonies shouted, to the cheers of the others in the Katikati village hall.

The Saturday night dance had become a frequent part of my life. Villagers flocked there on the weekends to float around the floor in time with the music – mostly American hits like 'The Tennessee Waltz'.

My head shook as I greedily gulped down another shot of whisky. It was giving me the necessary Dutch courage, and I was ready to weave my way across the floor and onto the small stage. The MC handed me an acoustic guitar which I strapped around my shoulder and faced my 'fans'.

'What do you want me to sing?' I slurred, a foolish grin planted across my face.

'Sing us, "My Cheatin' Heart".'

I strummed along with this hit by Hank Williams, then went on to a sentimental change of mood with 'Rocking Along In My Old Rocking Chair.'

With my performance over and the applause still ringing in my ears, I headed for the entrance. I don't know why but on my way out, I climbed up on the ticket counter and began to do a silly jig.

A few laughed while others shouted for me to get down. I heard my name being spoken from behind me. It was the local police constable. His words pierced my soul like a hot iron.

'Like father, like son,' he said disdainfully.

My voice started to tremble. What was I turning into? I seemed to be bound up in an intolerable web of destructive circumstances from which there was no escape. Like my father, I had begun my pathway to hell!

Chapter Three

'You Have to be Born Again'

A race with the wind seemed attractive to me. After all, danger and booze now combined to add spice to my ever more destructive lifestyle.

Still, the policeman's statement continued to haunt me. My father was an alcoholic and I hated it. Was I really so much like him? The answer was – YES!

I couldn't bear to see him weaving blearily alone along the road, but I was now following in his uncertain footsteps. Even though I knew the truth about his heavy drinking, I felt it was a family matter. So when I heard a man calling my father a 'drunken bum', I angrily punched him in the mouth.

Alcohol temporarily eased the pains for me, but it was also destroying me. I could not say 'No' to grog-filled adventures so when Doug, one of my mates, suggested that we go to a dance at Waihi Beach, I readily agreed.

'We'll go on my motorbike,' he said. 'Bring some grog. We'll need it.' Although my days were busy with cows to milk, work at the local sawmill, and trees to fell out in the bush, my nights were now my own, and I used them to drink myself into oblivion. I was burning the candle at both ends.

Laden down with gin, cheap wine and sherry, I rendezvoused with Bruce. A few swigs of sherry prepared us for the evening ahead.

'Let her rip,' I told Doug as I threw my leg over the seat of his shiny Triumph. I knew that our trip would be exciting as we careened along the winding, metal-based lanes to our destination.

Doug opened up the throttle and with dust and metal flying from the spinning rear wheel, the bike skidded to one side, then the other. Finally, with the machine under some control, we swerved around the first hairpin bend. I clung on for dear life, squealing with alcoholic excitement. Doug was a racing bike rider and under normal circumstances he could handle his machine well, but the drink had given him a false sense of bravado and blurry vision to boot. In his mind, this was some prestigious race in front of a large, cheering crowd. I closed my eyes and steeled myself against a rush of dizziness. We were soon cruising along at sixty-five, leaving a plume of dust behind us.

All went well for a few scary minutes, but then an S-bend on a steep climb proved too much for him. Doug lost control of the machine and as we became airborne, my world tilted up at a skewed angle. I closed my eyes as we sailed into the scrub as if in slow motion. Our trip through a void ended with a hard thud, causing spots to dance in front of my eyes.

Shaken, but still alive, I dusted myself off and asked my companion, 'What on earth happened?' We had both parted company with the bike which lay several feet away, it's engine still running.

'I don't know,' Doug said shakily over the sound of the bike's free-revving motor. 'Are you all right?'

'I think so,' I replied, as overhead a quarter moon struggled to make its way through the cloud cover.

I felt in my pockets and declared, 'Well, there's one piece of good news. The grog's still intact. None of the bottles are broken.'

With that, Doug picked himself up and was able to heave the machine back onto the road.

'Let's go, mate,' I told him, 'but this time be a bit more careful.

Remember, two other guys died on this road recently because of speed.'

My warning made little difference to Doug who was soon defying death again. Windswept, we pulled up at the dance hall in Waihi. I consumed more alcohol, pumping myself up with the kind of self-confidence that enabled me to overcome my shyness and ask girls to dance with me.

In the wee hours of the morning, we headed back. Doug opened up the throttle on a straight stretch of road. I don't know how fast we were going, but suddenly the engine died. Doug fought to keep the bike on the road as we wobbled to an uncertain halt.

'What's wrong, now?' I moaned, clasping my throbbing head.

'She's seized up,' he said. 'I reckon she's overheated.'

We were almost home, so he pushed the bike off the road and we were able to 'hitch' a lift for the final leg of the journey.

Even though we had survived this eventful trip, I knew it was only a matter of time before something terrible happened.

It did! That night, like all of my others, started in the usual way – with lots of drink.

'You wait there,' said Johnny to the group of four teenagers I spent most of my evenings with. 'I'll get the wagon.'

Johnny had been a delivery boy at the local bakery and had made a unilateral decision that the owner wouldn't miss his vehicle for the evening. He also knew how to jump start the Morris van. Johnny disappeared behind the bakehouse, and moments later, we heard the engine start. He then backed the vehicle around the corner to where we were waiting.

'Hop in,' he said. 'Hurry up! Let's get out of this place before we're discovered.'

We filled the wagon with our supply of grog and jumped in. The dance hall in Waihi was again our destination. Early evening had become the fading purple of late evening. Night was coming on quickly. As Johnny drove, we began greedily slurping down the potent contents of the bottles as if prohibition were about to come in.

'Watch out, Johnny,' shouted one of the group as the van shuddered violently. We were alongside a gorge and our back wheel had spun over the side. Fortunately, our momentum carried the vehicle back onto the road before a catastrophe could occur.

'That was close,' yelled Charlie. The laughter which had died momentarily, started up again and I nervously took another swig from the bottle. Mine was a high, helpless laughter, which was close to hysteria.

Suddenly in the darkness, a bridge appeared before us. Before Johnny could slam on the brakes, it was all over. Our front wheel was lying beneath the car and the sump had been ripped off, spilling oil everywhere. Smoke began to billow from beneath the hood.

'Get out, get out,' yelled one of the gang. 'She may catch fire.'

But we couldn't escape. The back door wouldn't open. The van was jammed end-for-end across the narrow bridge. Badly shaken, we managed to climb over the front seat and tried to force open a side door.

As we worked at it with all our might, the door suddenly opened with a rusty, hellish screech.

It was then that I felt an agonising pain in my left shoulder. I looked over at one of my friends and saw that blood covered his face. He had a gaping cut across the top of his left eye. A knotted bruise stood out on his forehead.

'We better get out of here,' said Johnny. 'If the cops catch us, we'll be in real trouble. We've got all this booze on board and worse still, we've pinched the van. We'll go to jail for years.'

Car lights appeared in the distance. *Who was it?* we wondered fearfully. The driver slammed on his brakes and a group of shadowy figures came running toward us.

'You Have to be Born Again'

'Are you guys okay?' asked one of them.

We were relieved to discover that it was some friends who had been following us on the way to the dance.

'Help us get this crate off the bridge,' I asked them.

Summoning all our strength, we heaved and eventually managed to lift the crippled vehicle to the side of the road. She was a total write-off.

'Let's get rid of the grog,' I told my friends as my head rolled woozily on my shoulders.

We loaded the bottles into two sacks, went down the road and hid them deep in the fern, planning to recover them at a later date.

Under the half-moon that stood out in the sky, we got a tractor from a nearby farmer and pulled the wreck into his paddock. We made arrangements with him to pick it up the following day.

Our night was completely spoiled, and worse still, the consequences of this fiasco could prove to be extremely serious for all of us.

Bloodied, frightened, and looking as if we had been in a war, we jammed into the other car and returned home. The mood was sombre as we began to sober up.

'What are we going to say?' I asked. 'We all need to tell the same story.'

We agreed that Johnny would approach his father who knew the baker and maybe, we hoped, they could work something out.

When the baker heard of the situation, his voice dripped with contempt for the bunch of us, but we discerned that it was just an act. Actually, he was ecstatic. It turned out to be a windfall for him. He claimed the insurance and made extra by charging each of us a certain sum of money for what he called his 'major inconvenience'.

We willingly paid up, and the police were kept out of the picture.

My life was twisting and turning in cycles of bad to worse, then back to bad again. I was hoping that things would settle down, but they didn't. In fact, they got even worse. A couple of weeks later while returning from the bush with some workmates, a load of logs tied onto the back of the truck, we saw the boss' three-ton Chevy off to the side of the road.

'I wonder where Gordon is?' I asked Pete, the driver of our vehicle.

Just then, Gordon, our boss, appeared at the gateway of a house, covered with blood.

'Whatever has happened?' asked Pete.

Tears were already streaming down Gordon's face. 'I've killed my baby,' he cried, overwhelmed with grief.

His daughter, four-year-old Kathy, had fallen out of the truck and gone under the dual wheels at the back.

We followed him inside and for the first time in my life, I was confronted by death in all its horror. There lay his beautiful child who had become a special part of our lives.

We had enjoyed her innocent zest for life as she had run freely among the woods and would throw her arms around our legs. Her face was now pasty white. She looked almost unreal, and her clothes were soaked with her own blood.

We stood there stunned. Strong bush men began to weep. Then Pete, our driver, began cursing God.

I don't think you're supposed to do that sort of thing, I thought, watching Pete shake his fist toward heaven.

God had no place in my life at that time, but I knew the things Pete was saying were wrong and I wondered if God would punish him for those statements.

For weeks afterwards, the heaviness of this tragedy hung over me.

On top of this, the bush work did not appeal to me. The dangers far outweighed the financial benefits. Almost daily, we would face some unseen hazard.

'You Have to be Born Again'

'Let the winch go,' I yelled to Gordon a couple of weeks after the death of his daughter. We were cutting down pine trees. The winch rope, hooked to a tractor, was secured to a tree that had already been felled. The tree began rolling down the hill towards some beehives that the boss had placed in the area. The rampaging tree crashed through the hives, destroying most of them and sending angry bees flying in all directions.

Now fully extended with the log continuing to careen downhill, the winch rope could take no more tension and the next thing I saw was Gordon flying through the air as his tractor rolled over, narrowly missing him.

The next day I was sitting on a felled tree that was hanging over a gully. I was removing the head from its trunk when the trunk began to roll and I fell fifteen feet into the gully.

The axe followed me just missing my head and slicing into my left leg. I felt an excruciating slash of pain at that moment.

My leg was deeply lacerated and bleeding. I lay there frozen with shock. That same day, Pete also cut his leg badly while trimming a tree.

What's going on? I asked myself. *Everything is going wrong. I can't take much more of this.*

With all these disasters taking place, I knew the time had come to resign from my job in the bush. To reinforce my decision, Tom offered my old job in the butcher shop back. I accepted, and it was a pleasure to get behind the counter again.

'Are you ready for the slaughterhouse?' asked Stan, Tom's brother. We were doing our own killing for the shop at that time.

A local farmer, Ray Yeoman, was a regular visitor to the slaughterhouse. He would come and collect the offal to cook for his pigs. He came in late one afternoon. Since I'd seen him working on a building site in town, not knowing what kind of building it was, I innocently asked him, 'When are you having your opening dance?'

'Oh, we won't be having one,' he responded.

Ray was a man of few words, so I didn't press him further. He left with his 'cargo' of offal and Stan turned to me and said, 'What did you ask him that for? He's religious! That's a church they're building.'

I wished I had kept my mouth shut.

The last waltz had ended and the band was packing up their instruments. I had met a lovely local girl named Jenny that night at the Saturday dance, and I planned to take her home.

I announced my intention to Harry, my companion for the evening.

'Oh, no, you're not,' he snapped impetuously.

'Who's going to stop me?' I replied, grabbing his collar. I was fighting mad. 'How would you like to go home with your head on backwards?' I gloated.

Incensed, Harry took a swing at me. Ducking out of the way, I crashed a right to his chin and he fell backwards onto the grass.

'Get up, mate,' I said, standing defiantly over him. 'Be a man and fight me.'

Lying there, his hand rubbing his chin, he said, 'Forget it.'

To the victor (me) went the spoils. I found Jenny waiting for me by the entrance to the dance hall. I escorted her to my Model-A Ford truck and opened the door for her.

The route home that night took us right past the church that Ray Yeoman was building.

They must have finished it, I thought, for on the outside wall there was a notice advertising the grand opening. It said, 'ALL ARE WELCOME.' I didn't know what we were being welcomed to but whatever it was, *it* was taking place the following night. Without thinking, I asked Jenny, 'How would you like to come with me to that?'

She smiled, her eyes brightening, and responded, 'Okay.'

That next evening, I drove to her house to pick her up and her mother came to the door. 'What do you want?' she asked tersely.

'I've made arrangements to take Jenny to the opening of that new church in town,' I said.

'Well, I'm sorry, but she's not going,' barked Jenny's mother with an indifference that chilled me.

Despite feeling let down, I was all dressed up and didn't feel like going back home, so I went to the church by myself.

As I parked my truck down the road, I could already hear singing. I crept into the hall and sat by the door, hoping that nobody would notice me. It felt strange. I'd never been to anything like this before.

The man next to me was singing at full volume. I didn't know the song. Church music was so different to what I was used to. Then, he left his seat and went to the front. Apparently, this man with a warm smile was to be our speaker.

He started telling about how God had changed his life. He said something about being 'born again'. This language was all new to me. He kept talking about Jesus Christ and how He died on the cross 'to save sinners'.

Something inside told me that he was speaking about me. 'God loves you and by accepting Jesus you can become a child of God,' he said.

I wanted to hear more, but was embarrassed to stay and ask questions so I left as soon as he had finished speaking. After I got back home and parked my truck, I went to my room and felt compelled to get on my knees and pray.

'Lord,' I began, falteringly, 'I don't know much about You, and I don't know where You are, but I want You to become part of my life. Amen.' When I stood to my feet, I felt that everything inside of me had been somehow turned around. An inexplicable joy suddenly flooded through my body. My years of exile from God were over, and I was free from the guilt of sin!

I returned to the church the following Tuesday evening. Don Caldwell, the man who had been speaking on that first night, met me at the door. I told him what I had done and he smiled broadly.

'You have been born again. You have been saved,' he explained. 'It's as simple … and as wonderful as that.'

His words actually meant something to me. I *was* changed. I could feel it. And to add to that joy, I knew these people really cared about me.

Soon, they began to invite me into their homes. I felt an important part of a new family. These folk seemed to be successful in every area of their lives. I had been desperately trying to climb out of the poverty syndrome, and as I began to read the Bible, I came across these words in 1 Timothy 6:17, '*…the living God, who gives us richly all things to enjoy.*'

The death-wish pattern of my life was finally broken. Great changes were taking place. My desires were changing. If only my grandmother could have been alive to see that day. *How many times she must have prayed for me,* I thought.

I longed to see others enter into this new life so that they, too, might know peace with God and the blessings that He brings. Even in those early days, my life was directed toward leading others to Christ.

I spoke to my friends quite freely about this new experience. 'I have given my life to the Lord,' I would tell them. But I soon discerned that they didn't want to listen and would keep their distance from me. I had found the purpose for living and wanted to share it with everyone. My life had been turned around 180 degrees.

I could not understand how I had missed this 'Good News' of Jesus Christ for so long.

'You Have to be Born Again'

When I told my father of this new experience, he was sceptical to say the least. 'It will last a month' he said. 'It's just a passing fad. You mark my words.'

But I knew this was not a fad. It was for real! I was even given the strength to kick the drinking habit, and my church family became a tremendous support team for me.

Reg and Elsie Harvey, for instance, had opened their home to me. They encouraged me in the things of God and in every way, they helped me in those early years of my development as a new believer.

After a few weeks, my father's view of what had happened began to turn to uncontrollable anger. He was being harassed at the local bar by his drinking buddies. One of the sullen barflies seated between the empty beer bottles had complained that I had become a 'Bible Thumper'.

My father cornered me the next day and said, his face flushed with rage, 'If you're going to carry on like this, you can get your blankets and go.' I could hear the venom in my father's voice. It looked now like I wouldn't even have a home. I stood frozen for a moment, puzzled over what he had said.

Fortunately, he never broached the subject again and for the time being, I stayed.

Chapter Four

For Better, For Worse

The pretty, young blonde conveyed an intriguing air of innocence as she swept past me at the door of the Brethren Chapel on that fine Sunday morning in 1953. My eyes followed her down the aisle to where she quietly slid across the pew and sat next to her parents, David Hockly and his wife, Marion. The rest of the family was seated there – her three sisters, Pamela, Merrill and Annie and her three brothers, Trevor, John and Peter. She carried her beauty without self-consciousness – with an easy, erect certainty.

I had been praying fervently for a Christian girlfriend, and when I saw this vision of beauty, I whispered to my friend, Horace, 'See her? She's going to be my wife!'

Horace looked at me, 'That's if you can beat me to her,' he chuckled, a twinkle in his eye. 'By the way, her name's Betty!' He seemed to gain pleasure from the fact that he had been able to relay this exciting piece of information to me.

During that morning's breaking-of-bread service as a succession of speakers stood and expounded from the Word, I found my thoughts and eyes being drawn towards the young lady sitting to the left of me. I kept trying to catch her attention, but she looked firmly ahead, apparently drinking in everything that was being said.

Now that I 'knew' who my wife was going to be (even though we hadn't yet spoken), I needed to find a way to spend some time with her. Betty left the hall before I could even approach her. I wanted this 'angel' to see my 1932 DA Dodge convertible. I knew it would impress her. However, she was gone, being driven home with her family in her father's 1949 Ford Sedan.

I spent the next few days trying to formulate a plan to get an invitation to the farm where Betty lived. I even drove the butcher shop's van there, hoping to catch a glimpse of my beautiful future bride, but she was nowhere to be seen.

When the following Sunday came around, Betty again whisked past me at the doorway without a flicker of recognition. A large, navy-coloured hat bounced jubilantly on her beautiful blonde hair as she approached a seat near the front. She knew exactly how to dress. After all, if your family had been in the Plymouth Brethren for three generations, you should know their 'dress code'. Why hadn't she noticed me? I had donned a dark suit in good Brethren fashion, and my slicked back hair was stiff with Brylcream. I had to find a way to speak with her so that she would at least know of my existence.

I was invited to lunch by two members of the church, George and Topsy Elliott. As I was the only Christian in my family, people from the assembly took good care of me on Sundays. I never lacked invitations. In conversing with the Elliotts, I broached my favourite topic of interest, Betty Hockly. After I had spilled the beans about my intentions toward Betty, I asked their advice on how I could visit her home – preferably that afternoon. To my amazement, I discovered that George worked on the Hockly farm so I challenged him, 'Surely you could find some excuse to get us up there.'

'I don't think you need one,' said George confidently. 'Let's just make a friendly call on the family and see what develops.'

So George, Topsy, and their three children climbed into his Bedford truck and headed up Wharawhara Road then along the jarring track to Betty's home. I followed in my sporty convertible. As we arrived, some members of the family had heard the noise of our vehicles and came out to greet us.

George gave me a nudge as we stood there in the yard, then he burst out laughing. I took his peculiar actions to mean that Betty probably wasn't there. I was bitterly disappointed, but still followed them inside for the ritual of afternoon tea, sponge cakes and biscuits. Surprise and attraction made my heart leap when I looked up and saw Betty standing there.

I was introduced to her by Topsy who said, 'Betty, my dear, I want you to meet the local butcher.' I winced, thinking that her knowing my profession would not help my romantic intentions.

I was right! She shook my hand out of politeness, then turned her back on me and busied herself with the preparation of afternoon tea.

Eventually, I was handed a cup of hot, steaming tea in a beautiful, fine China cup which sharply contrasted with the more common type of chipped crockery that I'd been used to in my home. Betty's father, a stately gentleman, launched into a monologue about the morning service.

'I thought Brother Kimber's exposition of the Word out of Exodus was excellent,' he stated. 'I…' His voice began to fade into the background as I locked my eyes on Betty while she circled the room providing more cakes, biscuits and tea for the guests.

'More tea, Eddie?' I was startled. Was she actually speaking to me? A dull, brick-coloured flush began creeping out of my collar. 'Err … yes. That would be very nice.' This was the first time in my life I had actually been at a loss for words. I felt my hand shake as she leaned over and poured the hot, brown liquid into my cup. Although I was tempted to devour all the delicacies arrayed before me, I tried to act like a gentleman.

All too soon, Betty's father announced, 'It's milking time and you'll have to excuse us. The old cows won't wait.'

I was let down, having hardly spoken with the ever-so-lovely Betty. At least she knew that I existed – even if it was only as a humble meat cutter.

As we made our way to the vehicles and drove away, there was only one thing on my mind, what could I do to capture her interest? Her image remained with me all that week – vivid and alive.

The answer came a few weeks later in the form of an underground adventure. Five young people from our assembly had planned a trip to the Waitomo Caves, and I hoped that Betty would be able to go with us. By the time of this outing, Horace had given up on Betty and was actually working with me to get her on this journey to the centre of the earth. Horace asked another girl, June, to accompany him, and she accepted.

'Why don't you use my phone to call Betty,' he suggested. 'Do it right now! The worst she could do is to say no.'

With perspiration beading my forehead, I dialed Betty's home number.

'Hello,' said a gentle voice at the end of the line. It was her! There was a difficult pause as I desperately tried to pull myself together. How should I start my invitation? I took a deep breath and launched into my well-rehearsed monologue.

'Betty,' I said, 'would you like to come with us to the Waitomo Caves on Saturday? There'll be a group of us going, including Horace and June.'

'I don't know,' she said in a non-committal way. 'I'll have to ask my dad.' I held my breath as I heard her muffled request for permission. I could make out her father asking who would be on the trip with us, and her reply seemed to take forever.

'Okay, dear,' I heard Mr Hockly say, 'but don't be late coming home.'

I was ecstatic with joy. At last I could spend quality time with this young lady who had been consuming all of my waking and sleeping thoughts.

That Saturday in 1953 had turned from apricot and amber into a dazzling full-blaze Spring day. We piled into a Hillman that belonged to one of the young people, Colin McLean. We bumped our way along the metal road toward the farm where Betty was waiting to join us on our adventure to the caves. I had planned that she would sit next to me as we rode along in the car. The fact that we would be cramped together in the backseat was an added bonus.

Once we arrived at the caves, I knew my moment was coming. We were going into the darkness to observe the glow-worms. Normally this kind of thing wouldn't excite me, but now I had someone very special to share the experience with. As we stepped into the river boat, I gently reached over to clasp her slender, delicate hand. Boy, what a moment! I felt like a whole new world was opening before me. Words seemed to be unnecessary for the rest of the day; in fact, I couldn't think of anything at all to say. We just held hands and my heart began to beat faster than I could ever remember. The glow-worms were just a backdrop for our romantic underground journey.

'Our glow-worms are quite unusual,' a guide told us. 'They are completely different from the glow-worms and fireflies found in other countries.

While most other glow-worms shine their lights as a mating lure, our type of glow-worm lights up to attract food. The hungrier it is, the stronger the light.'

'Now, please keep silent,' she added as we began our journey in the dark. 'The glow-worms extinguish their lights at noise.'

Our guide slowly pulled the boat by wires around a cornice and into a vaulted cavern festooned with thousands and thousands of pinpricks of light – each one so very tiny by itself, but collectively they were strong enough to allow me to see my lovely companion in the darkness.

It was a great day to remember in more ways than one. When we arrived back at Betty's home, I leaned over and these words came tumbling out of my mouth: 'I think I'd better put a deposit on a piano,' I said, having heard that she loved to play. Betty laughed, but I was quite serious. I could already picture her flying fingers playing hymns as I stood at her side and we sang together in our new home. Of course, my talk of buying a piano spoke of much more than just music. There was already such rapport between us. Once I'd made up my mind, I had no intentions of backing down.

Betty's lovely Christian family and the peace that reigned in that home was also extremely attractive to me. I so wanted to be a part of it all. Betty's father was a kind man and seemed to accept me as an equal. My family background could have made him fearful for his daughter's future, but he never voiced that concern and concentrated on encouraging me in the things of God. I learned more from this man than from any other single person. Each time I visited his home – which was pretty much daily – he would sit beside me and share with me from the Word of God. Mr Hockly was exceedingly wise and even sometimes seemed to be omniscient as he took every opportunity to impart the truths of Scripture to me. Perhaps he knew that this foundation would also bless his daughter in the days and years that lay ahead. His example was without blemish and his love for the Lord and the Word exceeded that of anyone else I knew.

As I witnessed the calm faith of Mr Hockly, I became desperately concerned for my own father who was on a rollercoaster experience of drinking and more drinking. It was a situation in which he seemed to be totally helpless.

After returning from the milking sheds one day, I knelt by my bed to pray for him. 'Lord,' I cried, 'I am willing for you to take my life, if you'll bring salvation to my dad.' I had such a burden for his soul!

I rose to my feet and suddenly realised what I had said. After finally becoming a vibrant human being, I was now asking God to take me to heaven. This brought me into another bondage, thinking all the time that God might actually take me at my word. For weeks, this fear overshadowed everything I did. When I could not bear the situation anymore, I went to see my friend, Reg, a mature believer.

After listening intently to my tale of woe, he shook his head. 'Eddie,' he said, 'do you honestly think you're good enough to pay the debt for your father's sin? The price has already been paid in full at the cross. What you are offering is worthless.'

With that, the cloud looming over me was lifted and I was able to release my father to God. He didn't need my 'help' to save him.

Not long after this, I heard a sermon at church on 'The Father Heart of God' in which the preacher explained that God is our heavenly father and loves us as such. Because I had not had a close relationship with my own father, I could not relate to this at all.

One day, while trying to come to an understanding of this concept, I felt the Lord speaking directly to me. 'Just scrap your father image,' He said, 'and allow Me to live My "Father heart of love" through you. I can do it, if you'll only allow it.'

What a release this was for me! Now I could again concentrate on my romance with Betty.

After my butchering day was finished, instead of going home where Ken, my youngest brother, had now entered the world, I did general farm work for Betty's father. I didn't mind a bit. It gave me more time to see Betty.

But then came another blow. I picked up the letter which carried the awesome heading, OHMS (On Her Majesty's Service), and I correctly guessed the worst.

Anxiously, I ripped open the envelope and there it was! I was being invited by 'Her Majesty' to appear at the Papakura Military Training Camp about 100 miles from home. There was no option but to go. The New Zealand Army had beckoned!

As a Christian, I knew this would be a time of great testing. I made up my mind right from the start that I would not be ashamed of my faith in Jesus Christ. I was bunking with forty other raw recruits. It was nearing 10 p.m. on our first night there, the hour I knew the lights would be turned off. *Should I get down and pray?* I wondered. *Or will I leave it until tomorrow?*

Beads of perspiration began to form on my brow. My heart pounded, adding to the discomfort that I already felt from the lump in my throat and shortness of breath. *No, I won't wait, I'll do it now,* I resolved. So dropping to my knees, I waited for the sarcastic comments to come – but nothing happened. Everything went quiet in the room, and I imagined every eye boring in on me. I don't think I prayed much. After five minutes, I got to my feet and as I climbed into bed, I was glad that I had honoured the Lord in front of these men. Nobody spoke a single word. My first big hurdle of communal army life was over.

When my heart finally stopped pounding, I opened my Bible and lay on my side to read it. By being consistent right from the start, I had apparently won the respect of my hut mates.

A few days later, I met a Christian from another hut. He confided in me that he didn't think there were any other Christians where he was bunking either, and that he'd been too scared to kneel and pray.

'Why don't you start tonight?' I said.

'I'll give it a go,' he told me, as panic flooded his face.

He reported to me the next day that he had knelt and prayed and been laughed to scorn. 'I won't do it again,' he pouted. The report of his experience made me glad that I had been a good witness from that first night.

The heavy discipline of 'boot camp' did not affect me as much as many of the other recruits. I guess it was because I had learned unquestioning obedience from my earliest days.

I was glad, however, when the fourteen weeks of rigorous training were over. I missed Betty so much, and had made up my mind that once I got home, I would find the right moment to ask her to marry me.

After two years of going out with Betty, I finally summoned up the courage to propose to her on her nineteenth birthday. However, it wasn't quite the romantic event that Betty had longed for. To start with, I had the flu that day and had taken time off from work because of the fever.

My joints felt like they were full of broken glass and my muscles ached terribly. But instead of staying in bed, I drove Betty into Auckland in my little Prefect 19 to buy her the diamond engagement ring of her choice. It was three hours one way. After we got the ring, I took her to the top of a large building. Auckland was built on seven or more extinct volcanos. From high above this beautiful city, we looked out over the Waitemata Harbour ('Sea of Sparkling Waters') and could see Rangitoto Island, a long, three-humped volcanic island whose shape never changes from whatever angle it is viewed.

With such a beautiful backdrop, I turned to her and said in a hoarse, cracking voice, 'Betty, will you marry me?' Betty's eyes danced with joy as she gently responded, 'Yes, I will.' Her face glowed with excitement. After slipping the engagement ring on her finger, I held her in a deep embrace.

Even while we stood above the harbour, my temperature had risen dramatically. I returned home in agony and went straight to bed, but was comforted by the fact that I would soon have Betty as my bride.

The following year, we finally locked our lives together. The date was June 23, 1956 when I stood at the front of the chapel where I had first heard all about Jesus Christ. Don Caldwell, the officiating minister, had tears welling up in his eyes. A lump came to my throat and tears also started to fill my eyes. As the organist played

Handel's 'Largo', I turned and saw Betty on her father's arm. She looked more beautiful than I had imagined. This veiled princess was about to become my wife!

Betty took her place by my side and Don began reciting the wedding vows. 'For better… for worse… in sickness and health… til death do us part.' These words were important to us because they were forever! Breaking up was not a possibility in our thoughts. As far as we were concerned, this was a lifetime covenant.

Betty and Eddie were finally one! For better or for worse! For Better, For Worse!

Chapter Five

Girls' Town

'Where are we going?' asked Betty as our car began to speed toward an undisclosed destination. We had managed to hide the 'get-away car' from my friends whom I suspected of planning to attach tin cans and toilet rolls to the rear bumper. I was determined that nothing was going to spoil our holiday. I had forty pounds in my pocket and I was determined to make this the honeymoon to end all honeymoons. I gulped when Betty asked where we were headed.

'I don't know! We'll just go by faith and see where we are guided,' I said, revelling in the joy of the moment of our magical mystery tour. Betty and Eddie's life of living by faith had finally begun.

I have to admit that it was an unusual honeymoon. I had planned to be away for two weeks, driving around the beauty spots of our country's North Island. I had never been in such a grand place as a hotel before and couldn't imagine how much one would cost. I learned quickly and after a few short days our meagre funds quickly dwindled. It became obvious that our honeymoon would have to be terminated much sooner than I had hoped.

How was I going to break the sad news to my lovely new wife?

Eventually, I worked up enough courage to broach the subject. 'Honey,' I began, in a halting tone, 'we have lots of things to do at home before I go back to work and I wonder if it might not be a good idea for us to head back a little early.' I explained that I thought it would be wise to hang on to the few pounds we had left to live on until my next payday which would be shortly after my return to work at the Katikati Butcher shop. Since it was midwinter and our car had no heater, Betty was wrapped in blankets. She agreed with my suggestion.

We arrived home with precisely five pounds and moved into a two-bedroom cottage on the Hockly farm. We had already painted and papered the cottage walls and I had planted a garden. Our furniture consisted of a table, five chairs and a bedroom suite.

With so little finances available and a burning desire to eventually purchase our own home, I sold my Ford Prefect and bought an old Army Indian Motorcycle for ten pounds. For the next two years, the ancient motorbike was our sole means of transportation except for Sundays when we would ride to church in grand style with Betty's parents in their car.

Regardless of the fact that we were constantly broke, we were tremendously happy. My dreams were slowly being realised. For the first time in my life, I could see potential for the future. I was going to own a home and planned to have my own business. I also had a burning desire to become a father, and it wasn't long before Betty leaned across the breakfast table, a warm smile lighting up her pretty face, and said, 'I've a funny feeling that we may be having a baby.' I could hardly believe it. There was nothing that could compare with the joy of that moment.

Because of my low income, I had taken a night job cleaning the post office and the local branch of the Bank of New Zealand. I bought a power mower and began a lawn mowing service, cutting an average of ten or twelve lawns every week. There was little time for anything but work.

Each Thursday evening, I would sit at my desk trying to balance our budget. In the area of finance, my father-in-law had taught me one thing – 'You attend to the outlet, and God will attend to the inlet,' he would constantly remind me. He provided a tremendous example in giving and always said, 'Ten percent is never yours. It belongs to the Lord. From then on, your giving begins!'

There was a time or two when I forgot to put the Lord's money at the top of our list of financial priorities. I would groan, repent, and begin again, making the Lord's tithe first, cutting back in other areas. Sometimes we would end up with as little as ten shillings for groceries and it seemed that we wouldn't make it. There were times when I went out to the side of the road and picked Scotch thistle or, as the Māori people call it, puha or Māori cabbage, and I would get watercress from the nearby river. I had eaten this way before, but it was all new to Betty. Over the years, God always provided, and we never once went hungry.

Our old motorbike was a faithful steed, but I felt so sorry for Betty as she froze on the 'backseat'. I'd lovingly wrap a cloth around it to try and make it more comfortable for her, but underneath was a steel frame and her rump never seemed to be free of uncomfortable bruises. Even through the pregnancy, as we bumped along, Betty would say to me, 'Well, dear, I'm just about holding the baby.'

The big day came on May 13th, 1957 – our first child began to knock at the door of life outside the womb. There was never a baby more welcome nor anticipated with more love than this little mite that was on its way into the world.

As the birth drew near, I asked my boss, Tom, if he would loan me the butcher shop vehicle each night in case of an emergency. He kindly obliged and when the time finally arrived, I drove Betty to the hospital in the Morris 1100 van with 'Katikati Butchery' emblazoned on its side.

The hours of labour went by very slowly. I rubbed Betty's back, trying to comfort her, but there was no comfort to be found as the excruciating contractions increased.

The veteran hospital nurse who was on duty at that time knew exactly what was happening and pushed me to one side, whisking

Betty's bed into the theatre. In those days, husbands were barred from witnessing the birth of the child, so as the theatre doors closed before me, I was left alone in the corridor with my thoughts.

I had planned to be really cool, and thought that I would be able to handle this episode with ease. After all, I was a full-grown man of twenty-two years. I returned the van to Katikati, then returned to the hospital on my motorbike. I was waiting outside the theatre, motorbike gloves clasped tightly in my hand, when the doctor emerged expressionless from the scene of the drama. He walked up to me and said, 'Mr. Cairns, you are the father of a healthy little girl.' Upon hearing those words, I felt all of my strength drain away from my body.

He extended his right hand to offer his congratulations, but I found my arms were completely limp. I was rooted to the ground – paralysed. My gloves dropped to the floor, and I began to quiver. I could scarcely form the simplest words of thanks as he added, 'You can go in and see your wife and baby now.'

My heart was pounding as I entered through the theatre door, and tears began to flow when I saw my beautiful bride and this wonderful little angel that God had given us laying in a crib beside her. Betty forced a weak smile and her lips quivered as she said, 'Eddie, she's really ours.' I walked over and picked up our child, holding her close to my heart. No one had ever had a child just like this one. Her name had already been chosen – Yvonne Joy. I had prayed for a son, but now it made no difference. It was to be my continued prayer throughout the years, that God would give me a son, but our next little babe which came fourteen months later was another beautiful little girl, Glenys Alexandra.

Betty and I enjoyed the three years we spent in our little farm cottage. I removed several rotting boards and replaced them. We built a garage. I dug a septic tank and put in a flush toilet to replace our previous one that was located out under the trees. We had a beautiful garden, and our home was rent-free. It seemed a shame to leave, but Betty was now pregnant for the third time and since we did not have a third bedroom, it seemed prudent for us to find a larger home.

Over the years, we had saved as much as we possibly could. In fact, we had put away eight hundred pounds – about US $1,600.

We searched out a nice home in the nearby town of Katikati and were able to purchase it for three thousand pounds. It was a white stucco house with all the 'mod cons' of the day. We had a large playroom for the children and I put together a playground for them in the backyard with a swing, a see-saw, and a sandpit as well as an old truck which the girls loved to 'drive'. This kept them occupied and happy in their new surroundings.

It was a joy for me to see Betty so elated about living in this new home with our two girls. God had blessed her with her heart's desire. It was the first home that belonged to us and it had everything that Betty and I had ever desired.

At night after work, Betty made it a habit to meet me, walking about three-quarters of a mile with one little babe in the push chair and the other on the tricycle. There was another babe in the womb, awaiting delivery. These were delightful days for us. My heart was full to overflowing when I saw these lovely, smiling faces coming toward me as I returned from an exhausting day in the workplace on my bicycle.

It had been the same at the farm cottage. As I had rolled up the drive at night on my motorbike, two little girls would be waiting for a ride before I parked the sputtering machine.

I would put the helmet on one and the gloves on the other and we'd ride across the lawn to the garage. Each evening, after a hard day's work, I was immersed in an overwhelming joy when welcomed by these beautiful family members.

In the midst of all this, I had one unfulfilled desire – to purchase my own butcher shop. After three years of living in town, such an opportunity arose. I made an offer for a shop at Waihi Beach, but it would mean selling our house to have the necessary funds. Thirteen months passed and I still could not sell our house. The shop eventually sold to someone else. Deep down, Betty had truly desired to remain where we were. She was organised and settled in our cosy home with our sweet little girls.

I became unsettled in my job. Tom, my boss, had told me that if I remained, I could purchase his business; however, he had hired his nephew and I felt that this promise would not stand. I began to make other plans to establish my own business.

After the butcher shop sold at Waihi Beach, I began to pray that the Lord would have his way in my life. I resigned myself to staying where I was at the Katikati Butchery, and gave up the struggle within. Part of my duties at the Katikati butcher shop were to make deliveries to Waihi Beach and I made many friends in that little community as a result. On my return from deliveries, I would often mow the lawn for one old lady and pray with another. Throughout my seven years there, I shaved an old man and cleaned him up. He was an alcoholic dying of cancer.

On one occasion, I even helped to castrate a cat for an elderly couple who had requested that I perform the necessary surgery on their tom. I agreed to do so and as I arrived at the end of my delivery that day, they were ready for the 'surgeon'. I could not believe the nervous state they were in over what was to me such a minor operation. I quickly took up a razorblade and wound the cat in a blanket.

I asked the man of the house to hold the cat for me. He went a lighter shade of grey and vanished into the next room, leaving his wife to be my reluctant assistant. She was very agitated which made it difficult for me to perform the operation. Her husband stayed behind the door, popping his head out now and then to say to his wife, 'Hold him tight dear – hold him tight.'

With anguish in her voice, she responded, 'I can't! I can't!' I tried to calm the distraught lady, assuring her by saying, 'It's okay my dear, it won't take a moment.' I quickly removed the two little particles of annoyance. Within moments, their precious cat had recovered from the indignity of the experience and was chewing on some ground meat and drinking milk. He had come through the ordeal a little sore, but unharmed.

I arrived home shortly after this in my new Singer 1500 car. I was as proud as punch with my new vehicle. 'Hey, honey, would you like to come for a spin into town tonight,' I enthused.

She surprised me with her reply. 'I've got a funny feeling that we'll be going anyway,' she said. Seeing that I didn't totally understand what she had said, she added, 'By the way I'm feeling ... I think I'll need you to take me to the maternity annex.'

It wasn't too long before things got underway and within a few hours, Sandra Anne (Sandy), had arrived. Again, I could not believe that I had not received a son but of course, we quickly welcomed our little girl into the family with great rejoicing. For the following four years, we enjoyed the wonderful pleasure of these three lovely little ladies, and we were bonded into an extraordinarily happy family.

I felt at peace with my situation, but had a vague feeling that change was about to take place. Within three weeks, a man named Doug arrived at my home during my lunch hour and asked me if I would be interested in buying his herd of cattle (about eighty in all) and taking over his share-milking job.

He had been a friend of my parents and they'd told him that I was looking for another challenge.

Of course, I hadn't had much farm experience outside of the cowshed. From the age of twelve until I was seventeen, I had risen before dawn to milk cows with my father and mother. I had begun working at the butcher shop at the age of fifteen. After completing my milking tasks, I would leave the cowshed at 7 a.m. Then my dear mother, who had now been replaced in the cowshed by my brother, Arthur, had always been ready with a hearty breakfast of porridge and bacon and eggs, or whatever other meat I brought home from the shop. She knew I needed to be on the job no later than 7:30 a.m.

After working all morning, cutting up meat, making sausages, etc., I would leave for the killing shed about five miles away where I would usually slaughter a couple of beef, half-a-dozen sheep and perhaps a pig for the following day. Then at 4 p.m., I would leave to return and milk the cows.

It had been a difficult time, and after Doug's visit and the offer of the farm, I felt it was something I could learn quickly. If I could sell the house, I would be able to afford to buy the cows. I agreed to take the job, pending the sale of my home which had already been on the market for thirteen months. Driving home from work the next day, I offered a ride to the local postmaster's wife. She told me her husband was retiring and they needed to buy a home of their own.

I told her of ours. The following morning the couple visited us and although raising the finances to buy our house was difficult, they managed – so our house was sold. I resigned my job and took my reluctant wife and three little girls to the farm which was situated just outside of Te Puke. I left thirteen years of butchering on Friday night, and after packing our belongings into boxes, I became responsible for eighty cows on an eighty-four acre farm on Saturday morning. I certainly needed the Lord's help.

The first night in our 'new' home was devastating. We had placed a mattress on the floor in a room reeking of mildew. All night I fought off large rats that scampered around us and sometimes, even over us. Every now and then, a rat would get caught up in the blankets. When that occurred, Betty would jump out of bed, pleading with me to 'get rid of the thing!'

Half asleep, I would jump up and give chase to a huge rat with grey-streaked fur and ugly, staring eyes as big as a healthy six-month-old puppy! The vile 'thing' would squeal in terror as it escaped from the room. The noxious smell of mice and rats permeated the house, including every cupboard. This was not a very good introduction to farming for my dear wife who never had a desire to go back to the land. It was the beginning of many hard years of work. I told Betty of my plan to stay for three years and then buy a shop, but it was fourteen years before we returned to the city.

The landowner promised to sell me the farm at the end of my three year contract, but it didn't take long for me to realise that this man was going to give me a difficult time. The machinery I was able to purchase for the job was dilapidated. I remember that the first year I would cut one round of hay then get off my tractor and kneel and pray that God would give me another clear round. So it went until I had completed the whole field.

Betty helped me with the milking. She looked like a spaceman having donned a mask, goggles and gloves. She was allergic to cows and suffered terrible hay fever attacks whenever she got near the shed. During her first year of milking, Betty became pregnant again. *This is it!* I thought. *Our son is finally on the way.*

Betty felt somewhat different this time. Everything was pointing to change, and I was convinced that my little boy was finally on his way. I drove Betty to the Maternity Annex in Te Puke ten miles away. I then took the other children to my parents and returned to the annex to await the arrival of my son.

Betty was having a difficult time giving birth and the hours went by slowly. I became increasingly concerned as staff ran frantically in and out of the theatre, but I could not make any sense out of what was going on. At last, a doctor emerged through the doorway and moved toward me.

He said to me, 'It's about time you changed your pattern. You've got another daughter.' I was shaken. I moved toward the theatre door and entered the room, trying for Betty's sake to look excited. She said nothing. Her body had taken a tremendous beating and she was extremely weak. I looked to the side where my beautiful new little daughter lay, a smile on her face. Her little fist was waving in the air as she looked up at me and I felt like she was saying, 'Daddy, I tricked you.'

I smiled at her and began to weep. Feeling desolation and bewilderment, I wondered if God would ever give me the son I desired. I kissed Betty and my little baby goodbye, then headed home to milk the cows.

I was overcome with tears several times that night as I worked alone in the cowshed. There was a deep cloud over me. I knew I shouldn't feel that way, but I did. It was then that I heard a voice (I am sure it was the voice of God). 'If you don't want her, I can take her back,' He said plainly.

I was ashamed and cried out, 'Oh no, Lord! She's a perfect child. There's not a mark on her. She's a wonderful blessing. Please don't take her away!' Immediately upon finishing the milking, I hastened home, removed my gumboots at the door and went to my bedside to kneel down and pray. I thanked the Lord from the depths of my heart for this new little blessing He had given us. I apologised to God, 'I'm sorry Lord, that I have felt so bad. I will never complain again.'

I rose from my knees feeling as if this crisis had passed and that all was going to be well. God was sovereign and His precious will had again been accomplished.

Our little girl, Marlene Ruth, had such a lovely personality that we began calling her 'Blessing' or 'Bless'. There was never a moment when she was not welcome in our home, but this great longing of my heart for a son had almost overpowered me.

Not long after Bless had been born, Betty returned to the hospital for surgery. Certain repairs were needed for damage that had occurred during the delivery.

Three-and-a-half years went by and I continued to pray daily for a son, but nothing had happened. Betty and I even spoke about adopting – perhaps a little Asian boy or some other little chap that might not otherwise have much opportunity in this world. But, in our busy life, we just didn't get around to it.

One night, as we lay in bed, I said to Betty, 'Honey, I feel satisfied with my four little girls. I think we'll just let it go.' We lifted our hearts together to the Lord. My prayer out loud was, 'Lord, I am satisfied with my four little girls and I thank you in Jesus' name.' That was it.

I believe the conception of our next child took place within a few days of that prayer. It seemed as though I needed to come to a place of thanking God for my four girls, and telling Him that I was satisfied before He could release this heart's desire of mine.

Nine months later, I stood at Betty's side in the theatre of the Tauranga Maternity Annex. She was under a specialist's care because of the operation she had previously undergone. However, this night, the specialist was handling a difficult birth in the theatre next door so a young house-surgeon was given the job of dealing with this delivery until the specialist was free. I became concerned when I noticed this young fellow was shaking like a leaf as he scrubbed his hands in the basin. This must have been his first time delivering a baby because he had a midwife at his side telling him what to do. I had been with Betty at the delivery of Sandy and everything was straightforward. Here things seemed tense.

'Cut her!' The midwife's voice was stern. He did, and blood spurted all over his white coat. 'It's not enough,' she frantically warned. 'Cut more!' More blood shot all over him. He put down the knife and took the baby by the head. Immediately it came forth, its bottom hitting the table. This young medic was swinging my baby by the neck! I had a son, but he wasn't breathing!

The young doctor stood frozen with fear. The midwife snatched the baby from the doctor's hands, put the suction machine into the baby's mouth, turned him over and slapped his bottom. He responded with a shrill scream, exercising his lungs as best he knew how. It was music to my ears. I don't think I ever heard anything so beautiful in all my life.

I had a son and he was alive, and he was the spitting image of his father. Glory be to God for his grace. We named him Gregory John. Betty's face was drawn, her eyes swollen from exertion, but we held each other and then our little boy. We were both so very happy. I had bought Betty a lovely sapphire ring and intended to give it to her whether she gave birth to a son or a daughter. But here, our baby boy represented one of the greatest joys of our lives.

Gently, I slipped the ring on her finger, remembering the very first time that we'd clasped hands at the caves, and I felt now that all of our dreams had come true. A special hand-picked little evangelist had been sent from the Kingdom of God to adorn our home.

The age of miracles had not passed.

Chapter Six

Thrust Me Out, Lord

Frost lay thick on the ground outside our farmhouse, and icicles clung to the guttering like fragile spears of crystal. The night was exceptionally cold.

I climbed out of the shower, filling the bathroom with steam like a deep London fog. It would have been nice to return to the fireplace and allow the dancing embers from the dying logs to warm my body, but I had been taught that we had to pray. I'd made the commitment and knew that I must go to the evening meeting.

I had always been faithful to this Wednesday night prayer-time in our Brethren chapel which was about a mile-and-a-half down the road from my home. The building was rather nondescript as are most Brethren buildings. A green carpet ran down the centre aisle of the sanctuary where people arrived silently and took their usual places.

It seemed the Plymouth Brethren had gone from being a revolutionary movement that traced its roots back to the evangelical revival in the 19th century, to being like many other groups that had then settled into a more comfortable routine.

However, I appreciated the strength of the Brethren which was that they had a determination to take Scripture rather than doctrinal formulas of ecclesiastical tradition as the norm. With the exception of a related group commonly known as 'Exclusive' Brethren who have developed eccentric doctrines, the Open Brethren subscribed to doctrines commonly held by a majority of evangelicals. The Brethren also stressed the unity of all believers in the body of Christ as well as their duty to propagate the New Testament gospel and live devoted lives. These were things that I totally agreed with. However, I had to smile curiously as I thought about what creatures of habit we had become.

Each week we would arrive cocooned in heavy, warm coats and mechanically sit in the same seats, in the same room, and pray the same prayers.

Not wanting to rock the boat, I took my usual seat about halfway down the hall. Brother Alf, as was traditional, launched into an intense opening – a very devout prayer – cutting through the stiff air of this poorly-heated room. Alf was a dedicated student of the Bible and was able to choose verses from all over God's Word and wrap them into his intercession.

After the initial prayer, he would quietly walk up to the pulpit and begin to expound the Word of God. He loved the Gospel parables and was quite an able communicator when it came time to clarify them and to give historical background of the time in which they had been written. He was always interesting and had a good repertoire of stories to tell. This evening, white vapour puffed from his mouth with each word, as he shared.

His task completed, Brother Alf retired to his seat and we opened the meeting for extemporaneous prayer. I tried to focus in on the prayers, but couldn't help noticing that the prayer needs never seemed to alter from week to week. There was one prayer that always stood out to me. It was a prayer that brother after brother (sisters were forbidden to pray out loud) would pray from the Book of Luke 10:2, '*Pray ye therefore the Lord of the harvest, that He would send forth labourers into His harvest.*'

This had always been a beautiful prayer to me but year after year,

Thrust Me Out, Lord

I never saw anything happen. Each of the brothers would say with feeling, 'Lord, we pray You, the Lord of the harvest, to thrust out labourers into the harvest fields.'

I never did see anything develop from the endless repetition of this prayer. One night, my heart was pricked. I began feeling that we had got it all wrong, so I stood up and boldly prayed, 'Father, thrust *me* out into the harvest field of the world.'

That prayer was soon to have a dynamic effect upon my life, but for the next few moments there was only dead silence.

Since there was absolutely no response – not even a soft 'Amen' – I wasn't sure whether I had done right as far as my brothers were concerned, but I sure felt different. It was the beginning of a renewed vision from the Lord. I had been labouring faithfully in church as the Sunday School superintendent for seventeen years but I now felt that my work was only my 'Jerusalem'. I needed to be out in 'Samaria and Judea and the uttermost parts of the earth'.

Another powerful spiritual event in my life began when my brother's ex-wife, Jan, shattered my sleep with a phone call at 2 o'clock one morning. The ringing broke into my slumber, and I instinctively picked up the receiver. Rubbing sleep from my eyes, I tried desperately to gather my thoughts as Jan said the stunning words, 'Arthur is dead.'

'Oh, Jan, where is he?' I gasped, in a sleep-slurred voice, clawing my way back to reality.

My younger brother had chosen to leave Christ completely out of his life, and only the Lord knew whether he had made the important decision to receive Christ at the moment of his death. My prayer and hope was that he did. Shock made me desperate to believe that he did.

I realised I was first into the world and that it seemed to me that I should have been first to leave it. I had lost my brother. I had piggy-backed him to school. We had played in the fields together, slept in the same room during our childhood years, and now I was faced with this great loss.

When I asked where he had died, Jan responded, 'His body was recovered from the Waitakeres (this is a range of mountains close to Auckland).' Arthur had been missing for five days and his body had been exposed to the elements. She told me that he had been out training, to regain his fitness. His plan was to walk right around the coast of the North Island of New Zealand with just a fishing line and a box of matches for survival. He had spent time in the jungles of Malaysia fighting the communists and knew how to take care of himself, so this was even more of a shock.

As I looked back on our years, I remembered a day when we sat together in our bedroom, and I had shared the Word of God with him. He had been so interested at that time, and spoken intelligently of the way of salvation, but he made no commitment to the Lord. When he went into the army, it seemed that he was robbed of every Christian value and from that time on, he appeared to favour an atheistic view of life and the world. Maybe I should have spent more time sharing with him… He left his wife and two lovely children behind, and my heart went out to them.

This and another incident laid even more of an urgency on my heart to win souls to Christ before it was too late for them. It was a shocking event that would never let me rest from the work of evangelism.

Betty had been dressing our children for Sunday School and I had gone off to collect some of the other pupils in my car. As she waited for me to return, she heard the squeal of a speeding car's tyres, followed by the sickening crash of metal ripping metal.

She ran outside and was confronted with a most gruesome, sad, and sickening scene. It looked like a massacre. Thirteen people were involved in a head-on collision. One vehicle was cut completely in half. Six of the thirteen already lay dead. Betty phoned the emergency services and gave explicit instructions as to what was needed at the horrifying scene.

As I returned from collecting the children for Sunday School to pick up my own, I was dazed by the horrendous scene. An old Māori couple with their children and grandchildren, used to come down to the beach to collect shellfish each Sunday. That day, they were on their normal outing when a group of seven young people who had been partying over the weekend, came around the corner at high speed. Although the old man had driven completely off the road in an attempt to avoid a collision, the young driver still failed to miss them. The old couple were killed instantly. Four of the youngsters in the back of the oncoming car also lay dead.

The police soon arrived with a doctor who had difficulty deciding which of the injured were the most serious – they were all so bad. Three ambulances were summoned, one from a distant city. We waited anxiously and prayed. Everyone was in desperate need of urgent medical attention.

I watched one young man begin to shudder sporadically. He tried to speak, but only spat while trying to force the sounds. It gave me a terrible feeling to see these people slipping into eternity right under my nose, but I couldn't reach them. I joined the police in carrying the bodies from the road into my shed to wait for the funeral director. Everyone was stunned.

'My life has been spent trying to prevent this kind of thing,' said the traffic inspector close to tears, 'but look at this … just look at this mess.' He turned his head to hide silent tears.

The driver of the speeding car, although badly injured, miraculously escaped death. The injuries were more excessive than I had ever seen. Traffic had been stopped, and several folks who approached the horrible wreckage in their cars quickly turned around and sped away. The few who approached the scene were speechless, totally helpless and shocked.

After the bodies had been removed and the injured rushed off to the hospital, I brought my tractor and front end loader out to remove the car that had been chopped in half. I towed the other car's remains off the road so that traffic could pass again. We washed as much of the blood from the road as possible.

After the funeral director loaded the mutilated bodies and drove out through our gate, I realised that my car – well back from the accident – still had children in it. By now Sunday School was well over and I returned the children to their homes, hoping they had not seen much of the deathly tragedy.

There had been several bad accidents on the S-bend outside our garden fence before and people had died, but we had seen nothing like what had confronted us that day. I felt so sad for the dear Māori families that had lost their innocent loved ones in this tragedy, and we were able to share the love of Jesus with many of the relatives as a direct result of this tragedy. They were so thankful for our kind attitude toward them and for the gentleness and loving remembrance that we showed toward their dead, that they accepted our words with open hearts.

Having seen lives snuffed out in an instant, my fervour for reaching the lost increased – to tell everyone I knew … and those I didn't know … of the Saviour's love.

By then, farming had taken a grip on my heart. I enjoyed working with livestock and began buying pedigree cattle. I became a harvester contractor, bought several good tractors and equipment and began baling hay and cutting silage for many farmers in the area.

Before long, ever increasing financial security made it possible for me to purchase a butcher shop in Matamata, adding to my work load which already kept me very busy. But still, I had a strong sense of community responsibility and served on the committee for the Paengaroa School where my five children were being educated.

I was involved in the Federated Farmers and the Parent-Teacher

Association, but in the midst of all this business, the Lord's work was still number one. I was superintendent of the local Brethren Assembly Sunday School which was made up of approximately one hundred children, and I taught the Bible in the public school one day each week. I made it clear to each of the farmers where I contracted work that one day a week at 12:00 noon, I would stop my machinery to teach the children. It only seemed fair to give each farmer the option of changing contractors for hay harvesting. They never did, and we never lost a bale of hay.

I felt this tremendous need within to share the Gospel, the good news that had come to mean so much to me, that Jesus Christ loved the world. He had died on Calvary's cross and shed His precious blood to wash away my sin. When I repented of my sin, He gave me the priceless gift of eternal life and the glorious hope of His coming as He did to all of His people, and I was one of them. That great hope never left my thoughts.

From my earliest days as a Christian, I put Scripture in the local paper with my name beneath the verses. This had drawn many phone calls which resulted in many visits to homes in the vicinity, sharing the Good News with all who were interested. I was compelled to get the Word out as much as possible.

In the Sunday School, we would give gifts such as erasers for school and balloons with verses of Scripture printed on them. We taught the children many memory verses. Later, I began to buy Bibles – at first only ten but then up to fifty at a time.

Each person that came to my home whether he was the milk truck driver or an insurance agent, would receive a meal, and a loving talk about the Gospel. A Bible was tucked under his arm as he left.

One morning in particular, a handsome, young salesman from the local dairy company showed up on my property. His brisk knock at the door made me eager to see who it was.

'Good morning, Mr Cairns,' he began. 'Today, I have with me a revolutionary product that will stop your cows from bloating.'

I looked at his product. He was carrying it in a tin container that was bent and looked rather abused. I asked if he had heard of anyone using it. Hanging his head and shuffling his feet, he admitted that he hadn't.

'So you don't know anything about your product,' I said pointedly.

'No, not really. I've just started with the company.'

Feeling sorry for him, I said that I would take some of it. 'Even though you know absolutely nothing about this product, I'll trust you, and try it.' Then I added, 'I have something that I have proven every day, and I know it works. It's a relationship with Jesus Christ.'

He stood speechless for a moment and his eyes fell back to the ground. Nervously, he kicked a stone on the ground. Then he lifted his eyes and said, 'My sister is a Christian. She never leaves me alone. I know she cares about me, and she keeps saying the same things you're saying.'

I suggested that he come inside for a 'cuppa,' and I shared with him from the Word for nearly two hours. On leaving with a Bible in his hand, he said, 'I think it's about time I took note of these things.' After walking him to his car, he sat with the door open for a time as if wanting to talk with me further.

Eventually, he started the car, and with a wave out of the window, drove away. I felt rewarded and grateful to God for that opportunity, and prayed that the young man's sister would continue to work until he too became a born-again believer.

The young salesman had hardly left the farm when another car hove into sight. Rubbing my hands together, I called to Betty, 'Honey, put the kettle on again. Here comes another.'

I considered that people coming to my gate were really opportunities that God was giving me to share the Good News.

The well-dressed man who came shortly after the dairy salesman was a Māori with a beautiful smile who promptly told me that he was an insurance agent for Combined Insurance. 'I understand that you are already with our company for accident insurance,' he said, 'and I want you to know that you now qualify for sickness insurance as well.'

It was close to lunch time so I invited him in and allowed him to present his product. After hearing all that he had to say, I took the initiative.

'Have you ever been born again?' I asked, having decided to lay aside any subtlety in my approach.

Surprised but not totally taken aback, he said, 'I have had a little bit to do with the Mormons.'

'But have you ever had a personal encounter with Jesus Christ?' I asked. 'Do you know him as your Saviour?'

It became apparent to me that he had not, so I said, 'My dear friend, I want to tell you about Jesus Christ and how He has changed my life and my desires.'

As we finished our conversation, I handed him a brand-new beautifully-bound bible. I said, 'I would like to give you this gift. Read it, and the Lord will truly bless you.'

His lips creased into a half smile, 'A friend of mine who came here one day last year, told me to watch out for you. 'You're sure to get a Bible as you leave,' he said. My friend was right!'

God had really been faithful in answering my prayer to… 'Thrust me out, Lord!'

Chapter Seven

Tortured for His Faith

I blinked twice, trying to take in what was before me. There was a giant of a man standing on the platform of the Tauranga Town Hall, stripping off his shirt and pointing out eighteen deep wounds covering his body – wounds of torture.

'These are the wounds I received for my faith in the torture chambers of Romania,' said the preacher in broken English but with a forceful quality in his voice.

This extraordinary man explained how in 1945, his country had been taken over by the communists, and he had begun an underground ministry to the 'enslaved people' of Romania and to the invading Russian soldiers.

The compelling man was Richard Wurmbrand. We were spellbound as he explained that he and his wife, Sabina, were arrested after three difficult yet successful years of running the underground ministry. His wife worked in a slave labour camp from 1948 through 1951 while Richard spent those three years in solitary confinement.

'I saw no one but my communist torturers,' he said. 'After the first three years, I was transferred to a mass cell for another five years where the torture continued.'

I looked at this man and knew that his eyes held more pain than I could comprehend. While Richard was being held and tortured, diplomats of foreign embassies had asked the newly-formed communist government about his status. The diplomats were told that he had fled the country. At the same time, the secret police told a contradictory story. Posing as released fellow-prisoners, they told Richard's wife that he was dead and that they had attended his burial in the prison cemetery.

'My family in Romania and my friends abroad were told to forget about me since I was dead,' he said.

After eight years of initial imprisonment, Wurmbrand was released and immediately went back to his work with the underground church in Romania. This resulted in his second arrest and a twenty-five-year prison sentence.

He was released with general amnesty in 1964 and once again continued with the dangerous underground ministry. Christian friends of the preacher realised the uncompromising danger of a third imprisonment and negotiated with the Romanian government for his release from the country. The government had started 'selling' political prisoners for hard currency. The 'going price' for a prisoner was eight-hundred pounds (sterling), but Wurmbrand's price was inflated. It would cost two thousand, five hundred pounds for his release.

As I watched this 'living martyr' with his wounds exposed for all to see, I could only compare it with films I had seen of the Nazi prison camps in places like Belsen and Auschwitz.

The hall was filled to capacity. As we walked from the meeting, no one spoke. The laughter and chatter that usually punctuated Christian rallies in New Zealand was markedly absent.

Instead, there was a stunned silence as the crowd of people quietly made their way to their cars.

It struck me that all of my life I had lived in a sort of 'down under' paradise, far removed from the rest of the wicked world. For me, New Zealand had everything from its sandy beaches and rugged coastlines to its calm green meadows and ominous, smoking volcanos; from flat plains and placid lakes to high snow-capped mountains and bubbling hot mud pools. There were even icy glaciers that crept down into sub-tropical rain forests ... and we had the freedom to enjoy these wonders and to thank God for them openly.

Even the Second World War had passed without scars on our beautiful land. Of course, many of our soldiers had died while in the Northern Hemisphere fighting in the war against Hitler, and deep scars remained within the hearts of mothers and wives who had lost their sons and lovers. But our land itself was untouched, and we were free.

As I returned home that night, the experiences of Richard Wurmbrand and others like him weighed heavily on my heart. I knew that I could no longer remain on the sidelines in the battle to help my brothers and sisters in Christ who had to survive under such oppression. I began giving substantial amounts of money to Richard Wurmbrand's mission, Jesus to the Communist World. I also gave to another mission that worked behind the Iron Curtain but began feeling that New Zealand needed its own ministry to directly aid the suffering church.

How could this be? I was just a simple farmer living in a country that couldn't be further from the rest of the world. However, I had to acknowledge that God does take the weak to accomplish His task. In 1975, the turning point came. It was prompted by a meeting at Faith Bible College, Tauranga, with Swiss-born Rudy Lack, of Youth With A Mission, an international ministry that had been started by an American visionary named Loren Cunningham.

To illustrate his work, Rudy Lack showed slides of a YWAM outreach to the Soviet Union. To me, Russia was a vast, faraway land securely locked behind a cruel, solid Curtain of Iron. One of the pictures revealed a Bible delivery point in Moscow. As I watched, I felt my heart leap and my finger reflexively point toward the picture. Almost silently, I breathed, 'That's what I want to do.'

After the meeting, I spoke with the pleasant Mr Lack, and he informed me of some of the exciting clandestine activities taking place in Eastern Europe.

'What can I do to help?' I asked.

He was excited about YWAM Slavic Ministries ran by Al Akimoff, a man born in China of Ukrainian parents. He revealed that this young ministry had many needs. I took out my checkbook. During a time of prayer, I had received a strong impression that the Lord wanted me to give an offering to aid the suffering church. I hadn't heard an audible voice, but I felt that it was to be a $1,000 gift. That was rather large for me to handle all at once since my bank account was already overdrawn, but I knew it was the right figure.

I had already donated some money to another ministry, so I wrote Rudy a check for $200 – then I thought of the $1,000 total that I was supposed to give. So I took out my checkbook again and wrote another check for $100. This still left me far short of the thousand, so I filled out yet another check for $100 leaving me with just enough for a project that would dramatically change my life.

As I prepared for my 'quiet time' the following day, I felt strangely uneasy. I kept thinking about what I had seen the night before, and prayed, 'Lord, what is it You want me to do? Please show me clearly.'

Immediately, I saw myself starting a mission – or at least opening a bank account that we could use to direct money toward helping the special saints of the suffering church. I called Sammy Abplanalp, a Swiss friend who had been with me on the previous night.

We had spent many hours praying together for our suffering brothers and sisters, and I told Sammy I wanted to start such an account and that there would need to be two people to sign the checks.

'Would you join me in this?' I asked. He agreed, and I got to work with the preparations.

I visited my bank manager, Mr White, with whom I had spent many hours talking about the Lord. He was a clever and wise man – a good Anglican. I told him of our plans. 'Eddie,' he said, as he sat behind his large desk, 'I would do anything to have a faith like yours. Do as you wish, and I will back you all the way.' Even though this banker thought that this was 'a most unique move for a farmer,' his support was a great boost.

We had a further meeting with Rudy Lack seeking a name for the new mission. Rudy had a brainstorm. 'It's a mission to reach out,' he said, 'So, why not call it, *Mission Outreach!*' This had a good ring to it, so I agreed to the name.

At last, New Zealand had its first mission to the suffering church. We formed a Board of Directors starting with Betty and myself. We added Sammy and Evi Abplanalp, and Franky and Zoe Grant, a precious Māori couple with whom we had worked for many years in our prayer and Bible study group. The name, Mission Outreach, has come to fit our work even more appropriately as we have continued to reach out further and further to many remote lands and needs.

Our first year yielded an income of only $5,000 and much of that came from just a handful of us. Our financial breakthrough came in a most unusual way. For a number of years, I had cut up beef for people to store in their freezers. They would pay me and often gave me a portion of the meat in return for my work.

I had saved some of the money from 'breaking' beef when a missionary arrived in my home. As I heard of his work, I felt the prompting of the Lord to give him that money. The following day I received a check for the same amount from another source. To prove that I meant business with God, I gave the missionary both amounts of money – twice what I had originally intended to give. Within a week, I had received another check that covered the whole amount from a customer whose account was long overdue – I had given up on ever receiving payment. I was beginning to see the hand of God at work even in those early days.

I became aware that God wanted all of the financial gain from my 'beef breaking' to go into the work of Mission Outreach. To prove God's faithfulness, I stopped charging for 'breaking' beef and gave each of my customers the opportunity to have it done at no charge – or to give a gift that we would then send to the suffering church. Many folks, Christian and non-Christian alike, thought this was a great idea and gave gifts that were far above what was reasonable. Others came on the mailing list and continued to give to the work regularly. This financial source continued to increase and thousands of dollars were given for the mission during that period.

During the second year of Mission Outreach, we (the six board members) felt that the Lord was speaking to us to trust Him for an income of $50,000 for the next year, 1976-77. It was a bit shocking to us all at first, but as we continued to pray, the Lord showed me in a vision just how it would be raised. I 'watched' a great herd of cattle lumbering through a wide open gate. I knew that they were mine, and that if the mission did not reach the desired goal, God would require Betty and me to make up the balance ourselves.

Over the next twelve months, Mission Outreach received $26,000 in gifts leaving Betty and me with a balance of $24,000 to pay. We had a staff house on the site of the butcher shop that I had purchased in Matamata. That could be sold and the finances given to the Lord's work.

'Are you sure you've got it right?' Betty asked cautiously as I spoke to her concerning this matter.

I nodded confidently. 'Yes, honey,' I said, 'I'm sure. I believe God is teaching us to give and by doing so, to be examples in giving. Then we can expect others to follow us in this exciting adventure with God.

'He also wants to teach us believing prayer, and then others will follow our example. I believe He also wants us to GO! Only then will others follow into distant lands to encourage and equip the suffering church. We must do our part in obedience to the Great Commission of our Lord and Saviour Jesus Christ when He instructed us all to *"Go ye into all the world and preach the Gospel to every creature."'*

On hearing this, Betty was also convinced that we should sell the house and it was immediately put on the market. It took a while to find a buyer and we eventually let it go for less than the current market value. It was time to pass the money on so we sold it for $33,000.

One day as I talked with Betty about the mission, I told her that I had asked the Lord that very morning what my message to our own nation should be regarding the suffering church.

'Did you get an answer?' she asked.

'I did! The Lord gave it to me from John 6 where it says that Jesus fed the five thousand and commanded the disciples to gather up that which was lying on the ground, that nothing be lost.

'I immediately realised that God is not a waster of resources, and I asked Him if He thought it was fair that we only gave China, for instance, what was lying on the ground. I am now aware that is where New Zealand is spiritually – just sending off what is extra – what is lying on the ground, and we have to lead our countrymen beyond that concept.

We have to run with it and take these gifts to far-away lands!'

I paused for a moment and then continued. 'The next message the Lord gave me was from Genesis 37:12-14 where Jacob was speaking to Joseph.'

I picked up my well-worn Bible and pointed to these verses which I had underlined. *'Jacob said, "Do not thy brethren feed the flock in Shechem? Come and I will send thee unto them." And he said, "Here am I."'*

'I see several things in these verses, honey. First, Joseph was called and he was obedient. He was being sent, he prepared, and he was available to the command of the Father. In the next verse, it says, *"And he said unto him, 'Go I pray thee, see whether it be well with thy brethren and well with the flocks and bring me word again.' So he sent him out of the Vale of Hebron and he came to Shechem."*

'I can see here that, if we are to respond to this Scripture, we need to go out to these distant lands and see how it is with the shepherds (pastors), and the sheep (the believers), and bring word back to the Body of Christ in New Zealand.'

These passages of Scripture along with God's specific revelation became powerfully directive to Betty and me, and has never ceased to be a driving force in our Mission Outreach.

Chapter Eight

The Voice of God

A pained look of concern swept over Betty's face. 'Eddie,' she asked thoughtfully, 'Why is it so many of our friends are leaving the Assembly? There must be something in this new doctrine of the Holy Spirit that we need to take note of.'

Don Caldwell, the man who had officiated at our wedding, and Ivan Bowen, an encouraging brother who had visited my farm on many occasions to joyfully share with us what the Holy Spirit had done in his life, were being vigorously attacked by the leadership of our local Assembly for their views. Eventually both had been forced to leave the Brethren, a fate that befell thousands in New Zealand at that time. The problem, as I understood it, was based on whether the gifts of the Holy Spirit in 1 Corinthians 12 were for today and for all believers, or had only been for the early church. The Brethren claimed the latter.

Ivan, who for many years was a world champion sheep shearer, had only one person he wanted to speak about – that was Jesus Christ. On many occasions before he finally quit the movement, he visited me. The elders of the church had followed like detectives working on an important case to check out what he had said and to discover whether he had 'polluted' me with this 'new' doctrine concerning the Holy Spirit.

Their negative probings and Ivan's effervescent joy drove me to the conclusion that Ivan was onto something special – something quite revolutionary and most likely true. I was aware that the Elders had a job to do, but their 'witch hunt' seemed to me to be both unjustified and unfair.

Don Caldwell was the most loving and gracious man I had ever met. I never heard him speak a harsh word to, or about, any one. His life and works were beyond reproach as I saw it. When he was rebuked by people, he never retaliated, but kindly spoke the things he felt that the Lord had shown him from the Word of God. I knew Don was well-schooled in the Scriptures and what he had learned must have indeed been worth my examination.

One night, when he was being spoken badly about at a meeting at the Assembly, I felt compelled to respond in his defence. 'Why are you judging this man?' I asked, trying to keep my composure. 'The only thing he's really saying is, *"Nothing is impossible with God."'*

Through all of this, Betty and I began to seek a release in the Holy Spirit. We felt a need for the added power that the Holy Spirit was said to bring. One morning, as was our practice, Betty had gone to have her 'quiet time' in our bedroom and I was in the lounge. I had completed my daily Bible reading and prayer, and waited for Betty's appearance. But she never came out of the bedroom, so I left for work.

Later in the day, as Betty and I were talking, I could see that something about her was different. She smiled softly and said, 'I spoke in tongues today!'

I was taken by surprise. 'What happened?' I asked, falling into a chair.

'I was praying,' she explained, 'and all of a sudden I began to speak in tongues. I've been seeking the Lord for His touch in this way, but it still came as a shock when I spoke in this heavenly language.'

I was confused. *Why,* I wondered, *had Betty received this gift and I hadn't.* I began to struggle over this and argued with the Lord, 'I thought I was supposed to be the head of the household, but You've touched Betty and not me.'

Despite feeling heavy in my spirit, I still continued to seek this blessing. One morning, a number of weeks later, I was deep into my 'quiet time,' kneeling down to pray by a chair in the lounge, when all of a sudden, it happened! A new language began forming in my mind and I started to speak it out loud. It was an extraordinary experience. I didn't want to leave that morning, and I found myself continually singing and worshipping the Lord like I had never done before.

At last, I too had been able *To Catch the Wind*.

I knew that this was of the Lord and wished that Betty and I had entered into this closer experience with God much earlier. Sadly, we had been informed through our Brethren teaching that speaking in tongues was 'of the devil' and I had believed this. But I repented of such thoughts, loudly asking God to forgive me, for I realised I had actually been guilty of accrediting the works of the Holy Spirit to Satan.

The Brethren Assemblies had definitely lived with an open Bible and had taught the wonderful truth of the 'priesthood of all believers,' but now I felt they had stumbled at what appeared to be one of the most important truths of the Bible – the gifts of the Holy Spirit are for all ... and for today!

On discussing the subject with Betty, I began flicking through my Bible and came across a fascinating verse. 'Hey, honey,' I said excitedly, 'listen to this.' I read a verse from Acts 2:38, '*And ye shall receive the gift of the Holy Ghost. For the promise is unto you and to your children and to all who are far off, even as many as the Lord our God shall call.*'

I pressed on. 'Peter wasn't just speaking to those listening at that time, but it says at the end of this reading that this promise is for all time. So that means that it's for you and me!'

I turned to Acts 19:6, where I read, '*And when Paul had laid his hands upon them, the Holy Ghost came on them; and they spoke with tongues and prophesied.*'

I explained that this group was probably made up of Jews, but in Acts 10:45, it speaks of Gentiles who were also speaking in tongues. 'They received the gifts just as the Apostles had,' I said excitedly. 'I'm no longer confused. I can see this gift is for us and I intend to move out in the power of the Holy Spirit.'

A few mornings after this experience, I was entering the lounge for my morning devotions. Just as I placed my hand on the doorknob, I was startled by an audible voice saying, 'Ask Me to go to Israel.' I knew it was God speaking. I turned my face upward and said, 'Lord, won't you think I'm presumptuous?'

There was no reply, so I sat down and opened my Bible. I was feeling strange about hearing this voice, but found some comfort and direction in my reading which was found in Esther 1. It tells of the King putting on a six-month feast for the governors of his Kingdom. Then after they returned to their respective positions, the king called for a week-long celebration for the servants that had laboured selflessly over those six months.

Before reading any further Scriptures, I paused, 'Lord, I *am* a servant.' I read further that each of the servants was handed a golden goblet. It was their choice either to have it filled to overflowing or take only a part of the wine that was offered. I literally stretched forth my hand as though I were clasping a golden goblet and said, 'Lord, please fill my cup to overflowing.'

Excitement welled within me as I left my chair and went out to Betty who was washing the breakfast dishes. 'Honey,' I said, 'we're going to Israel.' She was used to my outrageous statements and just responded, 'Oh!' With that, she continued washing the dishes.

I searched impatiently for the telephone directory.

'Why do you want it?' she asked, bemused.

'I'm going to call a travel agent to see what it will cost for us to go to Israel.'

Betty slowly turned from the sink and looked at me. 'Are you for real?' she asked with a disbelieving look on her face.

'Yes! God has spoken to me. We're going to the Holy Land.'

Betty accepted this quite happily and began to plan her wardrobe for the coming trip.

Within days, Rudy Lack returned to New Zealand and visited our home. When I informed him of what had occurred, he said, Eddie, that's wonderful. Let me give you some addresses of our YWAM bases around the world.'

I held up my hand to stop him after he'd given us details of YWAM bases in about twenty countries. 'We'll only have about ten weeks to do this trip,' I laughed. 'If we visited all of these places, we'd be gone for six months.'

My cup was now full and running over. Our first missionary journey could not come quickly enough. Betty and I began to make arrangements for people to care for our children and to take care of the responsibilities of the farm for the time we would be away.

We quickly found family members who were willing to take care of the children. This was a great weight off our shoulders.

I had a good farm worker, Graham Luxford, and he was able to handle the three-hundred dairy cows and young stock that I had on the farm at the time.

I had just 'dried the cows off,' meaning they would not have to be milked again for nine or ten weeks, and I had planned that I would arrive home just in time for calving.

The great day arrived early in May of 1976. There were no dry eyes to be found as we prepared to depart. What a heart-tugging time it was for Betty and me to leave our children for the first time.

We had mixed feelings that morning as we drove out of the gate. This was the first leg of a long journey that would start at Auckland International Airport, take us across Europe, and eventually on to Israel. After the formalities at the airport, we solemnly walked the long passage to the 747's doors and took our seats about halfway back in the huge passenger-jet.

I looked over at Betty. As our eyes met, she smiled and I put my hand on hers. 'Honey,' I said, 'did you ever dream when you married me that such things could happen?'

She squeezed my hand and continued to smile a sweet, heavenly smile.

The plane began moving from the blocks toward the runway. The engines revved, and Betty began feeling anxious. She was not a good flier. I noticed she was clenching her fists so tightly that her knuckles showed white. She had flown to Australia and had done some flying within New Zealand and still hated the experience of takeoff.

As for myself, I enjoy flying. I had taken up club flying for a number of years and had learned to pilot Cessna 150 and 172 aircraft. After touching down, I was always ready for my next flight. To me, flying is like being a Christian. Every time you leave the ground, you enter a new dimension. You are subject to new laws and your communications are through the air.

To me, it represents lifting into the heavenlies on the winds of the Holy Spirit as it says in Ephesians 2:6, *'And [He] has raised us up together and made us sit together in heavenly places in Christ Jesus.'*

The plane was racing down the runway, soon to part company with the ground and lift skyward. In a matter of seconds, we emerged from the cloud cover into a breathtaking world of uninterrupted blue sky. An incredible blanket of cotton-wool clouds lay just below us.

Betty gave a visible shudder and muttered through clenched lips, 'I hate this business. It seems silly to me that so many people would give their eye teeth to do this and can't, yet here I am – scared stiff.' With a nervous chuckle, she added, 'And it's costing us a fortune.'

Our first stop was Hawaii. We had a long wait in Honolulu for our next flight, so we took a trip around Waikiki Beach and viewed a few of the sights, including Pearl Harbour. We took an afternoon flight to the 'big island' so that we could visit the YWAM base at Kona.

It was most interesting to sit in on classes there and listen to the Discipleship Training program. We also took time to fellowship with the Kiwis attending classes there.

Our short stay in 'paradise' was extremely enjoyable, but it couldn't begin to prepare us for what was to come next! We were about to penetrate the menacing Iron Curtain of Central and Eastern Europe. Our great adventure with God was about to begin. Little did we realise that this was to be only the first of many.

Chapter Nine

A Giant Prison Camp

Wearing a khaki military uniform and firmly gripping his automatic weapon, the grim-faced Hungarian border guard strode toward our car. He stopped at the driver's door.

'Take your passports over there,' he snapped, leaning in through the open window. He was a large man, well over six feet tall, with shoulders that seemed almost as wide as he was tall. His face appeared taut, angry and suspicious. He pointed with his weapon toward a dreary-looking building. Being acutely aware of the Bibles and other Christian literature we had hidden in the trunk of our car for delivery to believers inside this country, it was unnerving to know that we were so close to having our booty discovered.

The four of us – Betty and I were travelling with Sue and Mike, a young American couple – clambered out of our two-door vehicle and began to pray that God would protect our precious cargo by blinding the guard's eyes when the search was made.

At the border of this country that sits at the crossroads of central Europe with its vacant 'no man's land', the dogs sniffed around vehicles and guards appeared to despise all visitors.

I absorbed the surrealistic scene and thanked God that I lived in a country of relative freedom.

'What do you think they are looking for?' Betty whispered.

'Contraband,' I informed her, 'and, I'm sure that includes Bibles.'

We had heard of these notorious border crossings where tyres were taken off cars, and gas tanks were removed. If 'illicit' goods were found, the guard would confiscate the vehicles and the property. It was a time when I knew I needed to trust in God. No one else could help us now.

Once inside the small, dimly-lit building, we stood in line to be attended to by a menacing immigration officer who turned out to be a woman of rather large proportions. She suspiciously studied our passports, compared the pictures with our faces, and checked that each of our visas was in order. Without a word, she handed our documents back to us and dismissed us from the office.

We returned to our car where another guard strolled over and directed us to move our vehicle to an area just a bit further ahead where we could be checked out.

'Open up the back,' growled a guard, moving toward the trunk. I obeyed, but not before sending up a telegraphic prayer.

'Lord,' I whispered, 'we've come this far. I'm sure You'll take us right through. We bless your Holy Name. Thank you Lord for hearing this prayer, Amen.'

The guard began poking his fingers at our bags, trying to ascertain what was in each of them. Every few moments, his eyes would lock onto one of us as we stood watching. It was as if he were trying to spot any sign of panic in our eyes. His job was to intimidate, and he did his job well.

The seconds ticked by at an agonisingly slow pace as we waited for him to complete his examination.

Suddenly, without warning he smiled, took a step back, clicked his heels, and said, 'Thank you.' We were rooted to the ground, wondering what came next.

As if anticipating our concern, the guard, with his thin lips pulled into a half smile, said loudly, 'You can go,' waving us back into the car. Stunned, we moved rather slowly, so he repeated angrily, 'Go, now!!'

A Giant Prison Camp

We awkwardly climbed into the car but began to trip over ourselves, as if having two left feet. The drama was over, and we found it hard to believe that they had freed us to take the 'Bread of Life' to the people of God. *How dare anyone deny His people His precious Word?* I thought Hungary had seen so much suffering since the 1956 uprising which resulted in 80,000 Hungarians being killed. The people had suffered at the hands of the Soviet troops who had brutally occupied their capital city of Budapest and caused 200,000 people to flee to the safety of the West.

We had left Germany earlier that morning with our young companions. Sue was just eighteen years old and Mike twenty-three. They had been married only a few months and had joined YWAM to become involved in missions. Through Mission Outreach, we were able to provide the necessary finances for the trip which had been suggested and partially planned by Al Akimoff, the head of YWAM Slavic Ministries.

As several border guards stood watch in their ill-fitting attire, Mike turned the key in the ignition and our car's engine caught, rattled, and coughed, then finally roared into life. Would they really let us pass? Mike pushed in the clutch and engaged first gear, then edged the car toward the main highway into this historic land of the Magyars. We passed huge vehicles still being checked alongside the many small cars, and again thanked God that nothing had been discovered in our vehicle.

I smiled at Betty as the scenery began to slip by. We seemed to be watching a travel movie.

Being a farmer, I was astonished to see that the Hungarians were still ploughing with horses. The horse and cart also appeared to be a popular mode of transport along the narrow roads.

'Look at the age of that old dear working in the hay field,' I said to Betty, pointing to a woman with a large scarf around her head and tied under her chin. Her dress was covered by an apron.

It was as though we were in a time warp. Although Hungary was thought to be more liberal and progressive than many of the other Eastern Bloc countries, it was still repressed and materially lacking compared to the West.

Our destination was to be a village close to Lake Balaton. This beautiful lake, the largest in central Europe, has its shores lined with Baroque villages, internationally known spas, magnificent vineyards, and inexpensive restaurants. It was in one of these Baroque villages that we arrived hoping to find our first contact. We had an address, but road signs were scarce and we couldn't locate the house we were looking for.

A teenage girl suddenly appeared and ran along the road beside us. She questioned us in English, 'Who are you looking for?'

I paused, wondering if I should reveal our hand. She was such a pure-looking girl that I decided she must be a believer.

'Pastor Ungary,' I said.

She nodded, then stopped and signalled with urgency, 'Follow me.'

Mike turned our car around and headed back along the road, following the girl as she sprinted toward a large house. I noticed several people standing by the house, and they waved us onto the property. Following their instruction, Mike drove the car underneath the house into a garage.

As we emerged, we were engulfed in warm, joyous, tearful embraces by the assembled group.

'We knew you were coming,' said Palma, the pastor's nineteen-year-old daughter.

I was puzzled at how they could have known. We had not told them, and I was sure Al Akimoff had not called them to let them know of our impending visit.

She read my quizzical expression. 'We always know when people are coming because the Lord sends us the food in advance,' she explained. 'Just today, we received vegetables, milk, and some meat from an animal that had been killed in the neighbourhood. There was so much food we knew we would have four or five people come to visit us very soon.'

Palma and her sister, the girl we had met in the road, were the only ones who spoke fluent English. We were introduced to each member of the family including Palma's father.

With tears filling her wide eyes, Palma informed us of her father's constant harassment by the police. He had been a pastor for a long time and was a very bold man with a level of faith that had gotten him into constant trouble with the authorities.

'Papa's now under house arrest,' she explained sadly. 'He cannot leave the property before eight o'clock in the morning, and must return by four. He can never leave this village.

'He must also present himself at the police station once a month for six to eight hours of interrogation. They always beat him when he goes. To make it harder for him, they make my mother watch the beatings.'

We were to discover that this harassment was not exclusive to Pastor Ungary who stood silently by. It was also meted out to other evangelical pastors and leaders who were caught operating underground ministries. The communist authorities felt that if they could cause a shepherd to deny Christ, they could scatter the sheep.

Lenin once said, 'The purpose of terror is to terrify.' I discovered during this trip that the police had succeeded in silencing many of the Christian leaders through their terror tactics. It seemed to Betty and me that the whole country had become a giant prison camp. *How could they survive such pressure?* I pondered.

While talking with Palma, a young man struggled into the house leaning heavily on walking sticks. 'I would like you to meet my brother,' she said. The young man approached us very cautiously. 'He lost both of his legs above the knee when he was younger. He and a friend had accidentally set off a landmine in a nearby field,' she explained. 'His friend was blown to pieces and my brother ended up in this condition. At least,' she added with ironic gratitude, 'he's still alive.'

That evening Palma led us to a secret room that had been dug out beneath the house. She had invited friends from Budapest to meet with us. The 'congregation' sat on rough wooden benches, and those who couldn't find a seat stood erect.

I was asked to share from the Word of God so I opened my well-thumbed Bible to Genesis 37 and showed them that as Jacob had sent Joseph to see how it was with his brothers in Shechem, so also He had 'brought me to Hungary that I might share with my brothers and sisters back home how it is with you.' The assembled group clicked their tongues in approval on hearing this. While I continued to teach from God's precious Word, I struggled to hold back the tears. I sensed the open hearts of these suffering but courageous people.

We had a precious time together that evening. Toward the end of our time as I was praying, I had a vision. In it I 'saw' many buildings, some multi-storeyed. I noticed that small candles shone from a few of the windows and realised that they represented the few house churches in the land.

I continued to 'watch' and the candles began to multiply until there were hundreds all over Hungary.

I told the young men assembled before me, 'God wants to multiply His church in your country. The pastors are captives and the church needs workers. I believe God wants you to take responsibility for the spreading of the Gospel throughout the land. And as you do so, the churches will begin to multiply.'

Many in the group were weeping by now. Then, one of the young men spoke. 'God has already shown us that we must move out, but it is very costly and we are a poor people,' he said sadly.

A Giant Prison Camp

'We need more pastors, but we cannot afford to pay them.'

'If you had the money, could you do the work?' I asked, knowing that some of them had already been in prison for their clandestine Christian activities.

'Yes,' they answered firmly – almost in unison.

'I will see if we can help,' I said. 'What are your greatest needs at the moment?'

'We need five hundred Bibles,' one said.

'Five hundred hymn books,' added another.

'We do not have any concordances,' declared a third. 'If we had an English concordance and some electric typewriters, we could translate and copy much of the concordance for others.'

I took out a pen and paper and made a note of these requests, trusting that God would use Mission Outreach to meet these vital needs.

There was a lull in the requests, so I asked, 'What else do you need?'

The group whispered among themselves in Hungarian, then Stefan who appeared to be the leader of the young men said, 'We need a car, brother. We have a few old vehicles, but they will not take us the many miles that we'll need to travel to share the Good News with our countrymen.'

Our mission was still relatively young so we didn't have an abundance of finances, but I recognised these people's great needs were genuine. With total confidence, I spoke out, 'Within one week of my return to New Zealand, I will send the funds for all of these requests.' It was a real step of faith for me, but I knew there could be no turning back.

Before leaving that evening, we were able to hand out some of the 'gifts' we had brought with us such as Bibles and other Christian literature.

Without our knowledge, the young men had prepared an itinerary for us enabling us to travel further around the country for twelve more glorious days. We were able to preach and encourage thousands of Hungarian believers across the land.

During our travels, we called on an elderly couple. It was obvious from their clothes and their sparsely furnished house that they were poor in the things of this world, but their radiant smiles made it abundantly clear that they were rich in the things of the Spirit. I was amazed to see the man of the house take a bucket and send it 50 or 60 feet down an open well to draw water.

He brought the water inside to his wife who poured some of it into a 'billy' (an Australian term for a metal pot hung over a fire) that was strung over an open flame. As we eagerly awaited our steaming tea, the old gentleman gestured for us to follow him. He took us into a small room which was actually their 'chapel.' The pulpit was made from two apple boxes and decorated with a curtain. He spoke to Palma who interpreted for us. 'He would like you two to sing.' she relayed.

My eyes met Betty's as the old man produced an antique tape recorder. 'Whatever can we sing?' asked Betty.

'How about "*What can wash away my sins?*"' I replied.

Without any accompaniment, we obliged. Having heard that Russian tapes only lasted a short time before breaking and knowing that our singing sounded dreadful, Betty said, 'I sure hope this tape is one of those that doesn't last.' Our off-key singing didn't seem to bother the old man at all. Being sincere worship unto the Lord from a foreign brother and sister, it was beautiful music to his ears.

We had been travelling for a few hours and the time had come for nature to call. 'Where is the toilet?' I enquired of the old man. He pointed in the direction of a clump of bamboo in the garden. I had just made myself comfortable when I was startled by a loud grunt coming from behind me. I jumped forward, imagining I was being attacked by a wild beast. It was a relief to discover that there was some bamboo between the pig and myself. Even so, I quickly made my retreat.

It was a joy to 'take' tea with these dear Christians, both in their eighties. They said that because they were Christians, they did not receive a pension from the government. 'We're not complaining though,' added the old man. 'We have an excellent garden and at the moment, we are fattening a pig.'

I know, I've met him, I chuckled to myself.

'Also, people within our congregation share their abundance with us. The Lord faithfully provides for all of our needs!'

It was time for us to leave for our next meeting in a small town about three hours from Budapest. We were given an address, but Stefan who was driving us warned, 'We must leave our car well away from the meeting place. It's dangerous to draw attention to our gatherings.'

Unfortunately, the car did draw the attention of an inquisitive policeman.

'Why is this car so far from Budapest?' the officer asked abruptly while looking at our license plate.

'We are just visiting "family",' explained Stefan. Of course this was true as we were visiting the 'family' of God. At that, the policeman appeared satisfied and pursued the matter no further. We were relieved, and our time spent with these believers was truly blessed of God. Our next meeting was to be in Budapest itself.

We spent part of the day looking around this historic capital, home to over two million souls. The hills of Buda shot up from the banks of the Danube while the Pest side was an endless array of cafes and restaurants. Although it was once the site of a Roman outpost in the first century, the actual creation of the city did not occur until 1873 when the towns of Obuda, Pest, and Buda were united.

'The cultural, political, intellectual and commercial heart of the nation beats here in Budapest,' we were told by a Hungarian friend who guided us around this breathtakingly beautiful city.

The real charm of Budapest lies in unexpected glimpses into shadowy courtyards and in long vistas down sunlit cobbled streets. It was down one of these streets that we attended our next meeting.

As the sun began to set, we were heralded into the dining room of the home by Stefan. The centrepiece on the table was a Bible. We learned that this was Stefan's house, and that his family had served the Lord faithfully for many years.

'Our father, although he's now gone to be with the Lord, housed and smuggled many Jews out of Budapest during the terrible days of the "Final Solution",' Stefan explained. 'Adolf Eichmann was intent on rounding up and sending to the gas chambers, every Jew in the city. My father felt that he had to do something to help God's chosen people.

'I have lost count of the many occasions that we went short of food because of our extra "visitors." But many lives were saved because of the help my parents gave them.'

As I listened to their story, I began to see the irony of it all. Here we were, having smuggled Bibles through their borders and using their home as a secret 'hiding place' to store the Word of God. Still, in the past, they had defied authorities because of their faith.

A delicious meal of meat and vegetables followed by dessert and coffee was graciously put before us. We knew Stefan's family was sacrificing their own food to serve us this banquet fit for a king.

After we had finished, a knock came on the door and two men walked in, soon to be followed by a couple of ladies. Intermittently for the next two hours, people arrived in twos and threes. Eventually, there must have been about 100 people jammed into the two adjoining rooms.

Thick drapes adorned the walls to muffle the noise. Soon the group began to sing familiar hymns softly but with a wonderful

Hungarian flavour. They sang, 'The Old Rugged Cross' and 'What a Friend We Have in Jesus'. Their worship was so beautiful that it brought tears to our eyes.

Stefan's brother, Paul, had just returned from four years in prison – a barbaric punishment for his Christian activities. He could not speak English, but my heart was knit closely with his. I saw such a Christian heritage contained in the shining face of this young man.

Stefan whispered that Paul was to have been married just a few days before his arrest and that his sweetheart, Georgi, had patiently waited the four years for his return. Standing hand-in-hand, they made such a beautiful couple. I could see in her shining eyes, the adoration she had for Paul.

Paul then broke loose and began dancing on his own in a corner, and clapping his hands while singing a song in English, *'Free, free, free, Christ has made me free. I was blind, now I see – free, free, free!'*

As I watched Paul's ecstasy, I realised that he knew the true meaning of freedom. He lived in a country that had vainly tried to hold him in bondage, but he was truly free in Jesus and was determined to continue living for the Lord whatever the cost might be.

The people continued to sing ever more loudly. They could not contain the depth of feelings that accompanied their praises to the Lord. After nearly an hour of this, it was time for me to preach. I rose to my feet and noticed that Paul was standing right in front of me. I moved over to him, put my arm around his neck and began to weep. He could not contain his emotion and he also broke into tears. Soon everyone in the room was weeping.

Even though I had not spoken a word, I felt I had already preached my best sermon.

After the hugging and weeping had ceased, I started in with a testimony of my life in New Zealand and told them about some of its difficulties. I shared how God had called Betty and me to come to see how it was with the 'shepherds' and 'the sheep' in their country.

I allowed my eyes to wander around the room, then opened my Bible at Luke 5 explaining how the Lord had entered Peter's boat and had preached to the multitudes who stood on the beach. 'Jesus desires to enter your life and dwell within you,' I said.

I said that, at first, they had only pushed the vessel a little way from the beach. 'Many of us are only "shoreline" Christians,' I continued, 'but Jesus said, "Thrust out into the deep." It was there that they began to gather in the multitudes of fish. It is only when we invite our friends, other missions and ministries, to come and help us that we can receive a full vessel of fish.'

I knew by their faces that these Hungarian believers were with me. I knew I was not a deep theologian, but I could only pass on nuggets as the Lord revealed them to me, believing that He would take them and do a great work in the hearts of those who listened and responded.

We continued to travel the land, meeting many different people in several more underground churches. Most of the Hungarian families were large, with six or seven children. They were usually all present at meetings, and I noted that the children were always well-behaved.

I had recently experienced a release of gifts in the Holy Spirit and would exercise these gifts while praying for long lines of people. As I did, the Lord revealed wonderful things for me to share, bringing many smiles to the people's faces as they listened to the intensely personal revelations that God had given me concerning them.

Nearing the completion of our visit to Hungary, the four of us returned to Stefan's home. Stefan and his family had set the dining table for a breaking of bread service. We sat at the 'Lord's Table' with such an awesome feeling of God's presence. Tears flowed with almost every prayer and when it was time to hand out the bread, we each received it from the hand of our brother Stefan, then we stood and gave him a hug.

At the conclusion of the trip, I had an overwhelming love for these dear people so much so that I wanted to give them all that I had. I took off my jacket and handed it to one of the young men who had accompanied us for part of the journey. I had noticed him eyeing it. I gave my Bible to Peter, another brother of Stefan, since he was learning English. Every time I put it down, he picked it up and fingered it tenderly. That Bible later accompanied Peter to prison. One week after we left, he was arrested and was sentenced to six years' imprisonment. Thankfully, after much believing prayer, he was released after six terrible months behind bars.

I gave my camera to Paul knowing that he could sell it for $600. He said he would use the money to purchase and reproduce ministry tapes for the house churches.

When it was finally time to leave, we were torn – not wanting to say goodbye. A group of these special saints decided to lead us to the edge of the city in a car. They led us to the main highway and waved us in the direction of the Austrian border.

I felt so sad that we were leaving these precious people. God had bound us together in an extraordinary supernatural love. For the first time in our lives, we had seen with our own eyes and become ONE with the suffering church.

I peeked out through the aircraft window and could make out the New Zealand coastline spread out below. We had crisscrossed Europe and had walked where Jesus walked in Israel.

'Honey, there's Mount Egmont. Doesn't she look beautiful?' I remarked to Betty who was trying to wake up from the long flight from Manila.

'What a trip it was,' I said, 'I still cannot get the needs of those people in Hungary out of my mind. Now we will need to raise the funds to fulfil our promises.'

Soon the wheels of the 747 hit the runway with puffs of smoke shooting out from the tyres, then curling away as the pilot put the engines in reverse and applied the brakes.

We went through customs in a confused daze. 'In less than three hours we will be home,' Betty said with relief.

'I wonder who'll be there to meet us,' she wondered out loud. After completing the formalities, the doors opened and our hearts leapt with excitement. There was Yvonne, Glenys and Sandy. After tears and hugs all around, they popped a surprise on us.

'Hey, Mum and Dad, we know how tired you must be so we've booked you both into a nearby motel,' said Yvonne brightly. I gave Betty a panic-stricken look. We were completely broke and couldn't afford a cookie or a coke to stave off our hunger and thirst, so a motel room was out of the question. I had given away $1,000 in Hungary to pay police fines for some of the house church leaders as well as making some gifts to YWAM people in Europe.

Because all of our money was gone, we had been on an unplanned fast during our layover at the Manila International Airport. This lasted from 8 a.m. to 1 a.m. the following day when we boarded the Qantas flight to Australia.

'I'm sorry girls, but we can't stay in the motel. We're stone broke,' I said reluctantly.

'Don't worry,' said Yvonne. 'It's our treat. We've already paid.' What a relief it was for both of us. For many hours we slept and slept... and slept.

For all of my joy at finally stepping on New Zealand soil once again and in spite of the wonderful rest, I had one concern occupying my mind. How was my bank statement? Was there enough for me to send the promised funds to Hungary?

When I had a chance to look at my statement, I found that we would only be able to give $5,000. We needed $8,000 to meet the commitments that I'd made to the Hungarian believers. Within

A Giant Prison Camp

a matter of days, an unexpected check arrived in the mail. It was from Betty's sister, Merrill, and her husband, Gordon. Gordon said in the accompanying letter:

'Please find the enclosed check for $2,000 to be used in your ministry.'

That was almost enough to cover the cost. Several small checks arrived and by the end of the week, we had the desperately needed $8,000.

This major outreach was completed, but our ministry was only just beginning! It was an encouraging start.

Chapter Ten

War Manoeuvres in Albania

The ancient Russian prop-driven plane sounded as if it had a death rattle, as it jerked uncertainly and sputtered over Tirana Airport in the mysterious land of Albania.

In just a few minutes – precisely a year after our first trip to Eastern Europe – Betty and I would fulfil our heartfelt desire to enter the People's Socialist Republic of Albania. This was a strange country that had taken the teachings of Marxism-Leninism to their logical conclusion and officially declared God to be dead. Since 1967, all churches and mosques (2,200 in all) had been closed. Even the crosses on gravestones had been savagely destroyed.

Before leaving home, I had read that there was only one messiah allowed in Albania. He was Enver Hoxha, a man who came to power in November, 1944, promising his people a utopia. It wasn't long before he became the self-appointed WAY, TRUTH, and LIFE for Albania. To remind the people of his 'greatness', his sayings were put on every public building, his name inscribed on every hillside and mountain.

Betty and I felt a desperate need to pray in this, the poorest country in Europe. We wanted to claim this oppressed land for Jesus.

On our shaky approach to the airport, Betty peered out of the window, then gave me a nudge. We were seated on the right-hand side of the aircraft about a third of the way back.

'What are all those mounds down there on the ground?' she asked. 'There are dozens of them. They look like bunkers.'

I stretched to see what she was talking about. Directly below, I saw what appeared to be scores of gun emplacements.

'They sure are a friendly lot,' I commented.

Eventually, the plane from Budapest began its final descent and landed laboriously on the runway. After taxying to its resting place beside the shoddy terminal buildings (which were overwhelmed by a huge picture of Enver Hoxha), the aircraft screeched to a halt.

When the engines stopped so did the air conditioning. The temperature inside the cabin shot up. Soon we felt that if they didn't open the doors, we'd all suffocate. Eventually the doors were opened, but this only added to our discomfort as a wave of oppressive heat filled the cabin. Sweat rolled down my face and my white shirt turned a dark grey colour in circular patches under my arms.

'I hope they get us off this thing pretty quick,' Betty remarked. 'Otherwise I think I'm going to faint.'

Even as she spoke, a group of Albanian military personnel boarded the aircraft and began going from seat to seat checking visas.

'What are we going to do?' asked Betty uneasily. 'We don't have visas.'

'Don't worry, honey, we're only in transit,' I said confidently trying to console her. 'There'll be no problems.'

As I presented our passports, the surly woman officer began flicking feverishly through the pages. She was not happy with what she saw or, to be more correct, with what she didn't see.

'Where are your visas?' she snapped in a most unfriendly fashion.

'We don't have them,' I sputtered.

'How did you get here without a visa?' she shouted vehemently, her face hard as stone. 'Give me your tickets.'

The lady appeared to live in a state of perpetual combustion. It didn't take long for us to realise she was a venomous creature who would turn and sting at the slightest provocation. Her eyes were now ablaze with anger. I tried to tell her that we were only 'in transit' to Athens, Greece. As if needing moral support, she turned to a soldier dressed in an olive green uniform and heavy boots, a red star on his cap. He got the message and declared loudly, 'You cannot come to Albania without a visa!'

'But,' I tried to counter, my face and hair dripping with perspiration, 'we have our tickets to go on to Greece. Can't we at least stay until the next plane goes to Athens?'

'No,' was her emphatic reply. 'You will return to Budapest on this plane.' Her dramatics were beginning to pall on me.

I vainly tried to protest her unilateral decision. 'Madam, this was not my mistake,' I said with exhaustion in my voice. I was not told we needed a visa and the Hungarian airline people passed us through without question.' I stared at her for a moment, then settled back in my chair.

As I looked at these officials, I could understand why (in 1810) the British poet, Lord Byron, had described Albania as 'a country rarely visited from the savage character of the natives.'

By now, all the other passengers had disembarked, and we were feeling a sense of deep frustration.

Without warning, she ripped out the next coupons from our tickets which were to have taken us on to Athens.

The antiquated airport was not equipped to 'hook up' the plane's air conditioning while it was stopped at the terminal, and the temperature had reached sauna proportions.

We looked around the cabin. The Hungarian hostesses were still on the plane. 'Why don't you get off?' Betty asked one of them.

'Nobody except the pilot, is allowed off in Tirana,' was her reply. 'Remember, this *is* Albania!'

It seemed to take forever as they reloaded the plane with baggage, and new passengers began to board. The plane once again became a cauldron of steaming bodies.

'Praise the Lord,' I heard Betty whisper almost to herself as the engines suddenly sprang to life. 'At least now we'll get some air.'

But after a few cooling moments, the engines were cut again. The captain emerged from his cockpit and stepped off the aircraft. It seemed he was having a dispute with a member of the Albanian airport ground crew.

'What is wrong, now?' I heard Betty ask a hostess as she mopped her brow with a handkerchief. 'We have too many passengers on board,' was her exasperated reply. 'We are short of seats and the captain refuses to take off.'

'Maybe they'll let us stay after all,' Betty whispered.

A harried ground official came aboard and ordered everyone off the plane. Then pointing an emphatic finger in our direction, he said with terrible manners, 'You two stay there!'

We discovered the plane from Tirana to Budapest was already fully booked, and our returning on the same plane meant that two others would have to be 'bumped' from the flight.

Finally, the problem was resolved and we were able to take off.

White-knuckled as usual, Betty prayed out loud. Then with authority she said, 'Satan, you think you have beaten us, but we will return.'

As we settled down for the flight, I closed my eyes and let my mind race over the events of the last few hours. My muscles were cramped, and my mind hazy. It seemed so long ago that we had left Romania, but it was actually just the previous evening. We had driven from Budapest, Hungary, to Arrad, Romania, to meet a Christian brother who (we were told) had lain dead in the city mortuary for thirteen hours before coming to life again. We listened to him and taped his astonishing story. During our time with him, I turned to Betty and said, 'And you think I'm excited about the Lord. What about this guy!?' He told us that he had been to the gates of heaven and back. All he wanted to do now was to 'work for the Lord and then get back to Him.'

We left at around 3 a.m. and drove through the night, arriving at Budapest International Airport just fifteen minutes before our scheduled take-off time for Tirana. The Hungarian airline officials rushed us through the normal formalities, neglecting to see if we had the required visas for Albania.

I felt extremely sorry for the two people who had to lose their flight to Budapest. The irony was that they wanted to go, and we wanted to stay. However, we had accomplished our goal – praying in the land of Albania. Though we had not even been allowed to leave the aircraft, we still had done prayerful battle with the enemy as we sat in the empty plane waiting for our forced return to Hungary.

I was angry with the Devil – at the way he oppressed these precious people whom God loved so much. All too soon, we were back in Budapest. There we booked a direct flight to Athens that same evening and arrived there totally exhausted.

We were more than a little confused by the apparent disaster of the preceding hours.

'You know, honey, I think this happened because we got ahead of our prayer chain back home,' I observed.

Before we left New Zealand, we had gathered together a group of our closest friends who promised to pray for us 'without ceasing' while we were away. We had given them a rough itinerary, but this began to change which meant that they would have no idea exactly where we were on any given day.

'I believe the Lord kept His hand on us and preserved us from possible imprisonment in Albania,' I said.

Before flying to Albania, we had spoken with fellow Kiwi, Reona Peterson who wrote the book, 'Tomorrow You Die'. Back in 1973, Reona had been caught giving a Gospel of John to the maid in her hotel. After her arrest, the Albanian authorities informed her that she would be shot for the illegal act at dawn. Fortunately, she was not executed but instead was released and deported from the country. *If we had stayed, we may not have been so fortunate* – so ran my thoughts.

After a refreshing night's sleep, we headed out to see my nephew, Wayne Ritchie, and his wife, Adrianne. This couple were young missionaries based in Piraeus, the port of Athens. At their home, we were introduced to a girl named Lynn from Thessalonica. She was involved in covert Gospel missions to Albania.

Lynn sat erect when I told her that while at the Albanian Embassy in Budapest, Betty and I had prayed that God would deliver the Albanian people and 'bring down the tyrant, Enver Hoxha.' We also shared that we had later flown to Yugoslavia and made the trip to the Albanian Embassy to try to get our tourist visas.

While in the Albanian Embassy in Yugoslavia, we were welcomed by officials who were keen to induct us into a well-known Albanian habit.

'Have some vodka,' said one of them. 'It will make you feel good.'

I thanked them for their kindness, but said that I would prefer a non-alcoholic drink. I was tempted to share with them then and there the Good News of Jesus Christ, but realised that if I had done so, we would never have gotten the required visas. We still didn't get them. They said we needed to be there for one week before they could help us, and we knew that would be impossible because we had to move on. So since we were in Greece, we decided to hit the southern border of Albania with our believing prayers.

I took a flight to an airport close to the border, hired a car and drove to the barbed-wire boundary. Joining me was Wayne's father, Don, and Lynn who knew the area like the back of her hand. I felt the Spirit of God upon me as I lifted my hands toward Albania and began to pray.

The words of Psalm 2:8 state that the Lord has given us the nations for our inheritance, but first we have to 'take them'. We were in the process! Suddenly, my eyes were bright with excitement and the grey despair that filled my heart and mind a few hours earlier peeled away like the morning fog.

We returned our hired vehicle to its owner and rode a bus to the shore of the Adriatic Sea where we boarded a ferry to the island of Corfu. Once there, we climbed high on a hill littered with sheep and donkeys, and sat among the olive trees for the remainder of the day.

From our vantage point, we could see Albania clearly and could even hear the rumble of Albanian trucks. At the same time, there was a continuing crack of gunfire coming from Albania. The whole scene was quite unnerving.

Lynn pointed to the centre of the channel between Corfu and the adjacent Albanian coast. 'The waters are filled with mines,' she explained. 'All shipping that goes through the channel has to be aware of that.'

Lynn told us of a project by a Pentecostal church in England, to pack translated selections from the gospels in floatable plastic bags and drop them into the sea, hoping the currents would take them to the shore across the way. I was keen on this idea and wanted to see these packets, so Lynn took us to a church basement where they were stored.

'We must deliver them!' I said urgently. 'It would be great if we could get a boat and a sailor who knew his way around the mine fields. I guess it would have to be done late at night.'

Lynn introduced me to a member of the church, and when I shared this request with him, delight crossed his face. He said, 'I know just the man for the job. His name is Petros.'

We were introduced to Petros and showed him the literature. I told this incredulous man what I wanted him to do. His face drained of colour and his limbs turned to jelly. My eyes could follow his trail as he streaked through the door, never to be seen by us again.

Upon returning to New Zealand, I was still feeling angry in my spirit.

It was such a pleasure to be back in our home with our friends. John Oram, a local engineer, headed up the team of prayer warriors that had begun meeting in 1978. If there was one thing I had learned from John, it was faithfulness. I unfolded the drama of our Albanian odyssey to my friends at our Saturday morning prayer meeting.

'We learned an important lesson that day as we sat in the plane,' I told the prayer group. 'That is that we should never lose communication with our prayer partners when we are on courier trips. Never again will we travel without the vital covering that you provide with your prayers.'

After giving my explanation about our instant expulsion from Albania, God began teaching us specifics through our prayers and reminding us that our example was the Lord Himself. In Luke 4, Jesus said to Satan on the Mount of Temptation, 'It is written ..., it is written ..., it is written.'

As we started our 'spiritual warfare', we used the same pattern by quoting Scripture to the Devil. For instance, we would say, 'Satan, it is written, *"Greater is He that is in [Me], than he that is in the world"* (1 John 4:4). *"He that is begotten of God keepeth himself, and the wicked one toucheth him not"* (1 John 5:18). *"Submit yourselves to God. Resist the devil, and he will flee from you"* (James 4:7). *"I give unto you power (authority)... over all the power of the enemy"* (Luke 10:19).'

Over the years, we have made it a common practice to use the Word of God as a weapon that the Devil cannot resist. That particular Saturday as I stood to pray, the audible voice of God once again spoke to me, saying, 'Pray for the removal of the leadership of Albania.'

Many will not understand this phenomenon and so I feel I should explain it. In John 10:27, it clearly says, *'My sheep hear my voice.'* I believe that means what it says. In John 18:37, it says, *'Everyone that is of the truth heareth my voice.'*

I believe that if we walk in truth, we will hear God's voice. It may be through His written word, an inward impression or various circumstances, but it *can* also be an audible voice.

That day, I explained what had just occurred. I took out a map of Albania that I had been given at one of the Albanian embassies. Placing it on the floor, I stood on it and began to pray over Albania.

I was obeying the Scripture in Psalm 149: 8-9 which says that we should, '…*bind their kings with chains, and their nobles with fetters of iron… This right [honour] have all his saints.'*

I cried out to the Lord to 'bind the wicked leaders of Albania' who had forced their nation into total atheism. I prayed for the secret believers who were still there, we had been told. I asked the Lord to preserve them and to hear their cries. I prayed, too, for the expedient translation of the Word of God into the Albanian language and asked the Lord for an opportunity to take His Word across Albania's apparently impossible border.

While I was in this mode of prayer, I saw a vision of a flagpole around which the serpent (Satan) had curled himself. His head was at the top of the pole. I shared this with the prayer partners and we began to pray against the Devil. As this took place, I saw further that he was being consumed by fire from top to tail.

I said, 'Keep praying. We are winning a great victory.'

Soon, he had been totally destroyed.

The voice of God again spoke clearly. 'Put up the banner of My love,' He said. 'This nation has not known love for a generation.'

After I had finished interceding aloud, the others joined in, each one imploring God to intervene in the affairs of that abused nation.

The following Friday, John Oram called me and said, 'Eddie, have you read the newspaper?'

'No, John, I haven't,' I told him. 'What's the big news?'

He said that Mehmet Shehu, the Albanian Prime Minister for more than twenty-five years, was dead.

'Some people,' he informed me, 'believe that Enver Hoxha murdered him!'

Indeed, God had started to answer our prayers for the release of that nation. We continued to pray that Hoxha would also be removed since he was the man who had been directly responsible for most of the suffering and murders of God's people in Albania.

That prayer, too, was answered. On April 11, 1985, Hoxha died at the age of seventy-six after ruling the country with an iron fist for forty years. Hoxha was the longest-lasting, non-hereditary leader in the world, having been in power consistently since the country's liberation in November, 1944. He had outlasted Stalin, Mao and Yugoslavia's Tito.

Psalm 149 had proven true in its statement that it was the right of the saints to remove wicked leaders.

Since the days of our Albanian adventure, the country has miraculously opened its doors to the Gospel. One of the first people to go in with the Good News was Wayne Ritchie, my missionary nephew! The apostle Paul visited Albania on one of his missionary journeys, and it was recorded this way in Romans 15:19, '*And round about unto Illyricum, I have fully preached the gospel of Christ.*'

As I understand it, Illyricum (the former name of Albania) means joy. Perhaps at long last that meaning can be fully realised for a nation held hostage by Satan.

Chapter Eleven

Danger in the Land of the 'Great Leader'

In my peripheral vision, I spotted a soldier running across a flat-roofed building with his automatic weapon. I froze momentarily, feeling a certain sense of intimidation as he pointed it at us.

'Look out, Ivan,' I shouted. 'That guy on the roof has a gun, and he's aiming it straight at us.'

I heard a metallic click, but the soldier held his fire. Still, he kept the weapon pointed directly at us. Digging deep within himself to find the necessary speed and without saying a word, Ivan disappeared over the crest of the hill leaving me alone in the soldier's sights. I stood quite still while Ivan escaped for I was convinced that if I tried to join him, it would have meant a bullet in the back for one of us.

For what seemed like an eternity, I stood and looked down the barrel of the soldier's gun which was pointed unwaveringly in my direction. Then he lowered his weapon and waved for me to move on. I did, with great relief. *What an introduction to North Korea,* I thought.

It was a chilly winter morning as I pulled myself from the warmth and security of my bed. Saturday had come around again. My prayer warriors had gathered to intercede – this time they were praying for North Korea. As we prayed, God spoke clearly, saying, 'Ask Me to put your feet on the soil of North Korea.'

I was deeply burdened for this far-off nation that was so isolated from the rest of the world. North and South Korea had been divided since 1947. The Korean War which lasted from 1950 to 1953, saw American and United Nations troops fighting against North Korean and Chinese forces. In 1953, a cease-fire agreement coldly divided North and South Korea roughly along the 38th parallel with a narrow demilitarised zone separating the two. This caused North Korea to isolate itself almost completely from the rest of the world. Their only meaningful allies were China, the Soviet Union and Albania. Their 'Great Leader', Kim Il-sung, appeared to be a replica of Enver Hoxha in his style of control.

The North Korean church came under chilling persecution. We heard one story telling of a game that children had been taught to play. The children were secretly to go into their parents' rooms, look for a 'little black book' and report their findings to their teachers. The children innocently brought back the news of their findings, believing it was all a game and as a result, four hundred sets of parents were executed for having Bibles in their homes.

I knew it was almost impossible as a foreigner, to enter the Democratic People's Republic of North Korea, but the Lord had spoken to me, and I trusted Him to make a way. It was 1982 and almost no tourists were being allowed in.

I was aware, however, that a small crack was opening up for business enterprise with the outside world, and guessed that would be the only way I could possibly enter. What would I do? How would one start 'trading' with North Korea?

These questions and many others went through my mind as I left the prayer meeting that morning.

A few days later, the phone rang in my home. It was Brother

Danger in the Land of the 'Great Leader'

David calling from Manila. 'I feel the Lord wants us to put another team into North Korea. Would you be part of it?' he asked. 'I've just returned from there, and there's much more prayer needed within the land.'

I felt my heart leap. 'The Lord has already spoken to me, and I am making plans to go,' I told him. 'Your call is another confirmation.'

Shortly before this, I'd had the opportunity (along with other business associates) to purchase a company that was already legally established but not being used. John, a lawyer within this business consortium, registered a new name for the company. It was appropriately called Higher Enterprises, Ltd. Still, we needed an invitation from companies in North Korea to get a business visa, so Brother David forwarded addresses of several such businesses to me. We wrote to these people who in turn, sent us invitations to view their products.

It was seven weeks later that I arrived again at Auckland International Airport for a trip into the land of the Great Leader. I didn't know how I could obtain a visa, but I was prepared to step out in faith. I headed first for the Philippines, looking to God to open the way into North Korea. I was learning that when I move in obedience to Him, He will prepare the way for me.

As I came through the barrier at the busy Manila International Airport, I was confronted by a large crowd of smiling Filipino people. Most of them were there to welcome relatives who had been working abroad. Slowly I began pushing my way through the chattering throng when I heard a familiar voice.

'Hi, Brother Eddie! Welcome to the Philippines.' It was Brother David, grinning from ear to ear. What a wonderful sight it was to see him again.

The streets of Manila buzzed with hundreds of gaily-coloured Jeepneys (Jeep taxi/buses) and darting pedestrians. As I climbed into his car for the hair-raising drive, I said to him, 'Brother David, will you help me get my multiple visa for China?' To reach Pyongyang, the capital of North Korea, I needed to go through Beijing. This multiple entry visa would allow me to enter China and re-enter it on my way back from North Korea.

Brother David made the arrangements. I went to his office the following morning. His multi-national staff prayed with us for the acceptance of my application. My American friend arranged transportation for me to go to the Chinese Embassy.

I sat at a table and filled out the application. Within ten minutes, a clerk called me into an office and invited me to sit in front of a rather portly Chinese gentleman who smiled cheerfully.

'Mr Cairns, why do you want to go to North Korea?' the moon-faced man asked politely.

'I am seeking business opportunities there,' I told him in a placating manner. With an unfading smile, he took a large rubber stamp and banged my passport with it. He also validated another document, closed my passport and handed it to me.

'Here you are. Enjoy your stay in China,' he said.

I was overwhelmed with happiness. I had anticipated at least a day's wait but in just twenty minutes, the task had been successfully completed.

As I hit the street, I couldn't keep from saying aloud, 'Praise Your Holy Name, Lord, for Your provision of this visa.'

After a cursory inspection, the Beijing customs official handed my documents back to me and waved me through. My friend, Ivan (also from New Zealand), was accompanying me. We both heaved a sigh of relief as the thirty Korean New Testaments we were carrying in our suitcases had passed through undetected.

Now the major task lay ahead. I had my airline ticket for North

Korea, but no visa. We checked into our hotel with only four days to get that vital document. If we failed, the whole purpose of our trip was lost.

'Would you order us a taxi?' I asked the girl behind the hotel reception desk. 'I want to go to the North Korean Embassy.' She looked surprised but responded to my request.

The taxi took us to a large building in downtown Beijing. Ivan and I found ourselves hoping and praying for a good reception. We climbed the concrete steps to the main entrance. As we entered, I noted how bleak it seemed. The only splash of colour was a huge picture of Kim Il-sung dominating the reception area.

I noticed that the staff was wearing large badges with Kim Il-sung's picture on it. They looked so sad. *Why are they so fearful?* I thought. A telex, whose clatter filled the room, formed a background for the commotion.

Approaching the counter, I said to a man sitting there stiffly, 'Excuse me, sir, but I would like a visa for North Korea.' I showed him my invitation. He studied it briefly, then stood up and carried it to a nearby office.

I waited for about twenty minutes. *Why is he taking so long?* I wondered. When he finally returned, he gave me my papers, and said, 'Go to your hotel. We will call you when we have news.' His glance was apprehensive, and his voice decidedly cool.

As I returned to my hotel, I said to Ivan, 'I'm going to pursue this further. They may just keep us waiting and do nothing. We'll return tomorrow whether they notify us or not.'

I had a strange feeling this was going to turn into a real battle. Things had gone so well up to now, but judging by the attitude of the man we had just met, we could be in for a hard time. We filled the rest of the day by touring Tiananmen Square and the Forbidden City.

The following morning over a breakfast of hard-boiled eggs and toast, I said to Ivan, 'We'll go back to the embassy right now.'

As we entered the reception area, I was confronted again by my 'friend' who seemed surprised to see me again so soon. He walked toward me. 'I told you not to come back – that we would call you,' he said in a stern tone, almost shouting.

Holding up my hand to parry his anger, I explained, almost reflexively, 'We have such a short time before we depart for your country. I am anxious to receive my documentation.'

That did nothing to humour him. 'We have called Pyongyang and have received no reply from the company that invited you,' he snapped. 'You must return to your hotel and we will call you.' This bureaucracy began to smother me like a giant octopus. I tried to sense even a hint of sincerity in his 'promise' to call me at the hotel, but didn't find it. Surely this was a trick.

The North Korean turned his back on us and began talking to other applicants. Trying not to appear too disappointed, I decided to stay around a while. I could sense that everyone in this place was fearful, and I determined within myself not to be intimidated by any of it. Eventually we left.

As we pushed through the heavy doors, I said to Ivan, 'We have to keep praying. The Enemy is doing all he can to block us. We must trust God.' We were becoming more and more aware of the spiritual battle we were engaged in.

The following day, we returned to the embassy only to be told what we had been told twice before. 'We will call you,' said the official with exasperation in his voice. 'Why do you keep coming back?' By now the man was trembling in anger.

'Because I need my visa,' I said feeling my voice rise stridently. I was not going to be put off by this difficult man. I paced around the reception area and noticed that the North Korean staff was becoming agitated. Then I walked up some stairs, saying 'Hi' to everyone I met. All work had stopped as they watched me. After a couple of hours, I said to Ivan, 'Come on, let's get back to the hotel. We must pray.'

That evening we strolled through the sweltering streets of the capital city. 'Eddie, Eddie,' came a voice from behind me. I turned and to my amazement, there stood Frederick, a Chinese friend from Hong Kong. I had met him several times before when he worked with a mission that I had frequently helped.

He came back to our hotel and joined us in prayer that our visas would be released the next morning.

Having prayed earnestly and at length, we decided that it was time to get some rest. As I slipped into my bed and drew up the covers, I wondered if it would be possible to sleep at all. Tension was rising. We needed a miracle.

'Lord,' I prayed before dozing off, 'we have come so far. Surely, You will not let us lose this battle now.' The next thing I knew, it was morning.

We went down for an early breakfast. This was to be our last morning in China. Our flight to North Korea was due to leave at 1 p.m.

'Ivan,' I said, 'all we can do is move by faith. Only the Lord can do this thing.'

After packing our bags, we went to the reception desk and checked out. I was determined to press on, believing God that we would make it onto that aeroplane. We confirmed our flight at the hotel airline office which was supposed to be impossible without the visa, but they didn't notice our lack of documentation and quickly gave us our confirmation. We summoned a taxi and told the driver, 'Please take us to the North Korean Embassy and wait outside. We won't be long. Then I want you to take us directly to the airport.'

We climbed those all-too-familiar steps, swung open the door and were confronted by my 'friend'. His face reddened when he saw me. 'Why have you returned?' he sputtered.

'Why won't you give me a visa?' I countered. 'What is wrong

with your country? I am a New Zealander. I am not a threat to anyone.'

Then he interjected, 'We have not had a reply from Pyongyang so you cannot go.'

Holding my ticket, I responded, 'I have my flight confirmed.' With that I took a step closer to him. We almost touched noses in our eyeball to eyeball duel.

'What will you do if I won't let you go?' he snapped.

'I will stay here for another week until the next plane goes to Pyongyang.'

This obviously stunned him. He surely did not want this Kiwi walking around his embassy every day for another week.

'Wait here,' he said firmly and disappeared. He returned a few moments later with another gentleman who was rather more gentle in his approach. 'So you want to go to my country,' he said.

'Yes sir, I do.'

'For what reason?' he asked.

I told him that I was in China on business and felt it would be a good idea to 'take a quick look at North Korea and see what products you have to sell.'

He looked at my 'friend' without saying anything, and turning back to me, he said, 'I am the Ambassador. I have the last word. You can go!'

The underling who had been so difficult up to now, suddenly changed his attitude. I informed him that we had only ninety minutes before takeoff and the drive to the airport would take forty minutes. 'I will phone the airline and tell them you are coming and they will wait,' he volunteered.

Immediately, he instructed a young lady to complete our visas. I thanked him and within a few minutes, we were on our way to Beijing International Airport. As the taxi sped through Beijing's streets, my heart lifted to the Lord in thanksgiving. Although we had won that battle, we were now going into the 'jaws of the lion' so there was no time to relax. The drama was intensifying and we needed to hold fast to our faith in the Lord.

As the taxi whipped into the airport, I saw a couple of airline officials standing by who were resplendent with their Kim Il-sung badges proudly displayed on their jackets. I wasn't prepared for what happened next. As the bags were unloaded from the back of the taxi, these officials came and stood by them. 'These bags must go through the X-ray machine,' said one of the North Koreans bending down to take our suitcases. Reluctantly, we fell in line behind them. They lifted our bags onto the machine.

'Blind their eyes, Lord,' I prayed and held my breath as a trained expert studied the screen in front of him. Miraculously the bags passed without any trouble. The Bibles had not been discovered. Our prayer had been answered. Clearance stickers were placed on each suitcase, then they were put on a conveyor belt soon to be loaded onto the aircraft.

'Quickly, follow me,' said an official. 'The plane is ready for take-off. They are waiting for you.'

He quickened his step, and we struggled to keep up with him. We were the final passengers. Ivan and I handed our boarding passes to the stewardess at the bottom of the stairs. Before climbing the steps, I looked up at the incredible sight before me. It was the oldest Fokker Friendship aeroplane that I have ever seen still in service. The paint was peeling off, tar blobs were dabbed all over the fuselage and it was in a state of total disrepair. Boarding this aircraft was quite an unnerving experience. *Will it even get off the ground?* I wondered.

We took our seats on the less than half full plane. A well-groomed gentleman who I later learned was the East German Ambassador to North Korea, sat directly in front of us. His seat was every bit as threadbare as ours. *There's no such thing as first-class on this flight*, I thought to myself.

As if to punctuate my thoughts, the engines rattled and shook us as they came to life. Smoke flew in all directions, and the plane continued to shake violently. I hoped that the tar blobs would hold this machine together.

Soon we were in line to take off – at least, that was the plan. The old plane began rolling and after a minute Ivan and I sat up in our seats. 'What's happening? This thing doesn't seem to be lifting,' I said to my friend.

In a matter of moments, the rattles ceased and we were actually headed skyward. 'Wow! Look at that,' said Ivan. 'Our undercarriage has just missed the treetops.'

'Don't get too excited,' I said. 'We've got mountains in front of us.'

The plane appeared to know its way 'home'. As we flew up the valleys and passed the first range of mountains, we almost could have reached out and picked the flowers.

Just beyond the mountains, we could see the city of Pyongyang coming into view. Set in a valley and from this distance, it looked to be quite beautiful. My heart began to pound as I saw the capital city. *What will we face here?* I thought. Just two weeks before, I had read an article about North Korea in Time magazine, and it had really savaged North Korea's leadership because of its ruthless handling of the people. Being from the West, I hoped that the publication of such an article would not have any adverse effect on our stay here. The North Koreans did not like criticism of their regime, especially of their 'Great Leader,' Kim Il-sung.

After we landed, Ivan and I picked up our carry-on bags and headed for the door. I stopped when I saw a large crowd standing below. There were television cameras and young ladies bearing flowers. Perhaps we were more important than we anticipated, or were they going to arrest us on camera? We soon realised that this entourage was there to welcome the East German Ambassador and his team.

Danger in the Land of the 'Great Leader'

As I reached the tarmac, I was startled when a tall gentlemen approached and asked, 'Are you Mr Cairns?'

'Yes.'

'I'm Mr Kim. Follow me.'

Ivan and I did just that and were ushered into the terminal. Customs formalities took only a few minutes and fortunately our suitcases were not opened. We were here on official business, so would not be subjected to the usual scrutiny.

I was surprised to discover that we had been assigned a handsome, black, Russian-made limousine. Mr Kim told us he would be our guide during our visit, then suggested that we get into the back of the car. He jumped in the front seat with the driver.

We soon arrived at the entrance of our hotel. The guide helped with our check-in and asked us to surrender our passports for the week-long stay. Then we were shown to our room.

'At last we're here,' I said to Ivan.

He smiled and then whispered, 'I just checked outside the door. Did you notice that we have a guard?'

We were soon to discover that no one could hardly eat, sleep, breath, or even use the toilet, without a 'guard' observing it all. The next morning, we ate breakfast in a large dining room with just a handful of guests, most of whom were Russian. North Korean guards and guides were plentiful.

I said to Ivan, 'How can we give these Koreans the slip? Every time we get near that front door, they are tailing us.'

I glanced over to the left and said, 'See that small door? I wonder where that leads.' The next morning while it was still dark, we came downstairs to check the door. No one was around.

'Let's make a run for it,' I said. 'We've got our camera – let's see what we can photograph.'

We found ourselves on the main street as daylight broke. Nobody was following us.

'Let's move away from this place quickly,' I said. The city was coming to life and people were beginning to move in the streets. We noticed groups marching together, singing songs with great fervour. I later learned that these were songs of revolution honouring the 'Great Leader,' and that many loyal North Koreans sang these songs on their way to the workplace.

People were seldom seen alone. As they came from their side streets, they would wait until a group of people passed by, and would join the crowd. It was the same with the children. They walked together in precision, wearing navy skirts or shorts and white blouses with red 'kerchiefs of the Young Pioneer movement tied neatly around their necks. The children also sang with great vigour.

I was able to photograph a few of these marching groups, but whenever I tried to aim my camera at any individual, fear covered their faces and they ran and hid behind a tree or buried their heads behind walls and bushes. I felt sorry for these oppressed people.

It was during this extended walk that we were confronted by the soldier aiming his gun at us from the rooftop. As I looked up at the barrel of the machine gun, I thought of how easily this young man could empty his bullets into me. Regardless of the fact that there have always been lots of Russians in North Korea, I thought that the North Koreans had probably seen very few Western 'white faces' and that they had been trained to kill Americans from earliest days. I stood still for several long moments so as not to cause the soldier to panic, then slowly turned around and followed Ivan over the crest of the hill.

'That was a close shave,' I said when I found him standing beside a tree. 'Let's get out of here. That was too close for comfort.'

We made our way back to the hotel for breakfast thankful for the unusual photo opportunity. The following morning, we found that our 'escape route' door had been locked. Mr Kim informed us at breakfast that we would be making a visit to some government buildings. The reason for the visit was very unclear.

We arrived at the offices and were ushered into a room to meet some officials who turned out to be our interrogators. My throat tightened when I looked at the faces of the four gentleman across the huge, varnished table. We were asked to sit opposite them. A nod of acknowledgment came from each of the North Korean gentlemen. A glass of water was set before us.

'What is your business?' asked one of the men seated across the massive table. 'I am the director of a New Zealand company called Higher Enterprises,' I said. Then I introduced Ivan to the men. 'He is travelling with me as my understudy.

I didn't want them asking him questions because he knew even less about the actual business than I did. He knew nothing! 'We are interested, sir, in the products that you have in this country for export.' The man came straight at me with other questions.

'How many ships does your company own? How many thousand people work for you?'

I began to feel weak. I had neither ships nor workmen. He asked, 'How many million dollars do you turn over per annum?' I was losing ground fast. All I could see in my mind's eye was the prison doors slamming behind us.

As he asked the next question I whispered, 'Lord, I have nothing left.' Mr Kim, interpreted for me. I said, 'I beg your pardon. Could you repeat that?'

All of a sudden, the Lord reminded me of the promise He had given me the night before I departed from the Philippines. It was found in Jeremiah 1:17, '*…therefore gird up thy loins, and arise, and speak unto them all that I command thee: be not dismayed at their faces, lest I confound thee before them.*'

I wasn't even allowed to get scared – even though I sure wanted to!

Immediately following this recollection, peace swept over me. It was unreal. I rose from my seat and with a forced smile said, 'Gentleman, you don't understand my business. We are agents travelling the world. We gather up books and samples of products available for sale on behalf of other people. We then return to New Zealand and display the materials. When companies decide to buy, we receive a commission according to the bulk of products sold.'

I was relieved to discover that this was an acceptable business practice to them, and it served as a satisfactory answer. They stood and shook our hands, then said that they would supply us with the necessary documents. Still in a state of shock, and amazed at the great miracle that he had just witnessed, Ivan moved towards me and said, 'I wondered how on earth you were going to answer them. I couldn't think of anything.'

'Neither could I,' I replied. 'It was only the Lord. I opened my mouth and He filled it with words.'

We rejoiced and praised the Lord together as we walked across the courtyard toward our limousine. The main reason for our trip to North Korea was to pray there and claim this country for the Kingdom of God. We walked into a park adjacent to the hotel, accompanied as always by our guide. I read that morning in Habakkuk 3:8 that the Lord rode the chariots of salvation across the heavens. Never in my life had I read more of the Scriptures than I did during that North Korean trip. I was seeking to build desperately needed faith in those bleak spiritual surroundings.

As I sat with Ivan on a park bench our guide standing just twenty feet away, we quietly asked the Lord to *'ride the chariots of salvation over the land above us and to open the heavens.'* I called for Michael the Archangel and Gabriel to help us break through. I looked up and in a vision, the heavens began to open. At first, it was only the size of a man's head but as we prayed, it continued to enlarge until the whole of heaven had cracked open. I stood to my feet while caught up in this vision. The anointing of the Holy Spirit was undoubtedly upon us. We had caught the wind of the Holy Ghost, and we sensed that He was working His great and gracious works for this country.

As I kept my eyes fixed on the vision, I saw what appeared to be flower petals falling from heaven but as I looked closer, I could see that they were actually segments of fruit. The people began to pick them up and eat them.

'What is this, Lord?' I prayed. Then I heard the recognisable voice of God saying, 'This is the fruit of my love.' I was so encouraged! God, in His faithfulness, was opening the windows of heaven and pouring out His love on this needy nation, and they were receiving it.

On the final night, we secretly placed our cache of Scriptures in various strategic places close to the hotel. We knew that if we were caught, we would be staying a long time in North Korea – but not in a hotel! We left believing our trip had been successful for we knew now that God was about to move in this forsaken nation. But how?

In 1991, I heard of an extraordinary breakthrough in North Korea. A delegation from the William Carey International University in Pasadena, California, was invited to visit North Korea. As a result, the North Koreans agreed to establish a chair of Christianity at Kim Il-sung University, and they had already welcomed a visiting professor to teach the faculty about historic Christianity.

On top of this, they agreed to receive 4,000 Christian books for use by students at the university. They also agreed to study the possibility of inviting a well-known American evangelist to the capital city as well as former President Jimmy Carter who is a Sunday School teacher.

Since my visit, the first and only Protestant church in the North was opened in October of 1988. It belongs to the Christian Federation (KCF) of which 10,000 individual Christians are members.

Times are changing – even in North Korea.

Chapter Twelve

The Pearl of Great Price

'There's a typhoon coming toward us!' Captain Karl's voice resounded with frustration and anger as he addressed the crew on the main deck. 'The anchor won't hold our weight, and we're going to end up on the rocks!'

This was the final straw for Captain Karl. He had continually warned Project Pearl's leadership of the dangers that came with travelling during the rainy season. Those dangers had become a reality as a typhoon bore down upon our overburdened ship.

'We should have been out of here two months ago. Now we could lose everything!' he barked.

I agreed with the Captain although I thought ironically, *If the good ship* Michael *had left two months ago, I would not have had the privilege of taking part in this grand adventure!*

I turned on my radio to get an update on the weather. The static-filled broadcast warned that an approaching typhoon was only a few hours from Hong Kong. Things looked desperate for the mission.

Ivan and I knew there was only one solution – that was prayer. We completed our chores of cleaning toilets and washing dishes and went to our place of prayer in the lookout.

The morning was so still that it seemed unlikely – to the untrained eye – that a typhoon was about to hit. I had never experienced one before, but I knew that what the Captain had said was true. He understood the elements and knew all too well nature's potentially devastating effects on a sea-going vessel.

We needed a miracle or Project Pearl would be sunk!

'Lord,' I began my impassioned prayer, 'You know what our needs are at this time. You know of the impending dangers that we face. We need for You to deliver us.'

As I prayed, Ivan saw a vision. After it was completed, he turned and said, 'Brother Eddie, I saw a tunnel of light through the storm. I believe God is going to take us through in safety.'

Then as if to mock us, the wind began to whip up into a frenzy. The sky turned an ugly grey colour and the sound of thunder came to my ears. We hung on tight. It seemed as if the typhoon was about to unleash its fury.

'We have stirred the Devil, brother,' I said. 'Let's continue to pray.' We did and as quickly as the storm had come, the angry winds dispersed. Our prayers had been able to catch the wind and turn it away. Two hours later, a weather update on the radio informed us that the impending typhoon which had killed twenty-nine people in the Philippines, had unexpectedly veered off and was now heading for Taiwan.

God had heard our prayers as well as those of thousands of other believers around the world who had not been given details of Project Pearl but were being guided by the Holy Spirit in their times of intercession for us.

Brother David's large, strong figure climbed aboard the *Michael*. 'Not another meeting,' somebody remarked laconically when they saw him. There had been so much bad news and so many emergency meetings that the crew couldn't bear even one more.

As we gathered in the dining room, David stood up and

announced, 'I have some good news for you. We've had a call from China. They're ready for the delivery!'

His announcement was greeted by a stunned silence. It seemed too good to be true. 'We'll be leaving in two days,' he said.

Forty-eight hours later, we assembled in the wheelhouse to honour the Lord. Brother David had communion bread and wine prepared for us to celebrate together before our life and death mission. It was an extraordinarily beautiful morning. Each passing minute set off the pearl-grey dawn of our D-Day – the day we would finally lift anchor for China.

None of us knew what lay ahead. Until this point, we were secure in the relative safety of the Hong Kong harbour. We had read stories in the local papers of smugglers being shot by the Chinese coast guard off the shore of Swatow. This was to be our destination.

Before we broke bread, Brother David said to us all, 'If any of you for any reason wish to leave the boat, there's an airline ticket waiting for you on shore. There will not be any hard feelings. Everyone who comes with us today must clearly understand that this is going to be an extremely dangerous mission.'

There was complete silence. That was taken to mean that no one was quitting.

As we celebrated communion together, the mood was solemn. I thought of Betty and my children back home and was thankful to know that they would be well provided for should I fail to return. I looked at the younger men with their whole lives ahead of them and wondered what was going on in their minds. Some had young children. Mine were almost completely independent.

To me, taking communion that morning held more significance than I could remember. I considered this could truly be my LAST SUPPER. Thoughts of dying added great depth to my appreciation of God's goodness in my life and strengthened my total reliance on Him for the future. As the Lord had set His face toward Calvary, so we were setting our faces toward what could very well be a Calvary experience for us, too.

There was no turning back!

Captain Karl was agitated and was getting ready to move. 'Prepare to sail,' he told his motley crew. Except for him, not one of us were true sailors. Our journey up to the south China coast depended greatly upon the expertise of this self-confessed 'sea dog'.

We lifted anchor and Captain Karl allocated our duties. Mine was to steer the ship from 8 a.m. to 12 noon and from 8 p.m. to 12 midnight. *Why not?* I chuckled to myself. *After all, I am well qualified. I was a Sea Scout thirty-five years ago.* My turn at the wheel wasn't long in coming.

'Okay, Eddie, it's your opportunity to steer this thing,' said one of the crew.

'You teach me and I'll do it,' I said rather nervously. I held the large wheel and wondered out loud, 'I hope I can keep this tugboat on course.'

'Just keep your eyes on the compass,' was his advice. The captain had set our course toward the south tip of Taiwan so we would be several miles outside the main coastal shipping lanes. The sea was calm and by the end of my first watch, I was just about getting the hang of it.

When I retired from my watch on the second night, I lay on my bunk to sleep but sleep evaded me as I rocked to and fro with each movement of the sea.

So many things were whirling through my mind. After four hours, I was still wide awake. I closed my eyes still trying to fall asleep when suddenly a shudder shot through me as I saw – in my spirit – a serpent touching a wooden handle with his nose. I knew immediately that the serpent was the Devil.

I bolted upright in my bunk and began to pray with great urgency. I interceded for all the crew members and their families.

The Pearl of Great Price

The wooden handle was a mystery to me, however, so I prayed over every handle I could think of that was on board.

I had not thought of the handles on the steering wheel. Feeling there was nothing else that I could pray for, I lay back down on my bunk and continued wondering what this vision was about. Suddenly, without warning, the ship's engines cut. It was a warning of impending change.

While our trusting captain had slept soundly, one of our 'sailors' had misread the compass and taken us off course. His companion took the wheel and gave it a couple of healthy turns, thinking that he was correcting the problem. Instead, he put us on a collision course with the barge.

Totally panicked and confused, the two woke up the captain who was soon at the wheel. He yelled down a pipe to the Scottish engineer, 'Cut the engines!'

It was at this point that I jumped out of bed and was on deck within seconds. To my horror, I saw through the darkness that we were heading straight into the barge and that this situation was connected with my vision. If we collided, we would destroy the Bibles and the tugboat would probably be sunk by the impact.

In the nick of time, our captain was able to avoid the disaster. Once back on course, I returned to my bunk where I was finally able to snatch some sleep.

The Enemy had tried to 'search and destroy' our mission, but the Lord rescued us once again from what could have been a watery grave.

As we drew near our delivery point, we were each given a body belt with a waterproof bag attached to be tied next to our skin. We were instructed to place our passports inside the bag in case we were caught or shot.

Tensions were mounting steadily among the crew as we entered the large harbour at Swatow. Dusk had overtaken us and many fishermen were returning from their day's work. Ships large and small cluttered the ocean, all trying to nudge their way into the harbour.

'Pull up the barge!' shouted Captain Karl. It was at least 100 yards behind us and we could see a fishing boat heading directly toward the tow rope.

We heaved the large nylon rope by hand, closing the distance between the tugboat and the barge. In a few minutes, we had the nose of the barge up close to the tug. Fortunately, the captain of the fishing boat noticed what was taking place and veered off to port.

Keeping our voices low, we could hear the chatter of the Chinese on the nearby vessels and we didn't want them to hear us speaking English. Our eyes and ears were straining to catch the smallest sound that might betray us and to see anyone lurking in the shadows.

Suddenly one of our crew whispered urgently, 'There's a gunboat coming across our bow.' The boat was on our port side and was moving slowly through the water. We could see large guns mounted on the front and men standing with automatic weapons in hand at the stern. She was so close that I could have thrown a coke can on her deck.

'Oh, Lord,' I breathed, 'Please blind their eyes.'

As if talking to the gunboat, Captain Karl mumbled, 'If you don't look at me, I won't look at you.'

We waited breathlessly for her to pass. Then, as quietly as she had come into view – as if we were completely invisible – she glided past us back into the dark grey dusk.

As if that weren't enough, another problem arose. Looming suddenly out of the half-light came a huge ship. 'It's a troop carrier,' said Captain Karl. We were dwarfed by this huge vessel. We passed slowly. We were so close we could see the sailors on deck. Fortunately, we went unnoticed.

It was getting dark, but a full moon began to illuminate our way. The distant skies were rose-dyed by sunset, and the horizon became silver under the moon. We could vaguely see the shoreline and the channel pegs.

We sat outside the harbour awaiting a signal from the beach. There it was! One, two, three flashes – right on target! Captain Karl had never entered Swatow Harbour before. That night he used only his charts as a guide and did a magnificent job.

'Let down the anchor,' he called. I winced as the chain passed off the winch making a terrible grating sound that echoed in the darkness. The captain 'parked' the tugboat and the barge parallel to Swatow Beach which was about 200 yards away. She had settled in an ideal position for the unloading of our precious cargo.

The night was brilliantly clear. It was as if the Lord were burning a huge torch for us. The sea became still, almost like glass reflecting streaks and flickers from the heavenly light.

Captain Karl ordered that the sides of the barge be lowered and that each man be in position for his assigned task. We needed to lower the barge into the water since it had been specially built for this manoeuvre. There were 232 one-ton packages sealed in waterproof plastic containers and secured firmly with ropes. They needed to be unloaded. The plan was to sink the barge about four feet into the water allowing the cargo to float.

We had three French rubber Zodiacs built like military assault vessels and equipped with powerful outboard motors which were able to operate in shallow waters and even up onto the beach.

The idea was to tie several packages together and once they were afloat, the Zodiacs would pull them to shore.

'Start the pumps,' ordered Captain Karl. 'We haven't got much time.' The pump motors roared to life and the barge began filling with water. In just a few minutes, the packages were floating.

Once the Zodiacs were in the water, ropes were attached to the packages and with engines labouring, they began hauling their life-changing cargo toward the beach.

The first Zodiac hit the beach and people – like bees around a honey pot – began to appear from nowhere. We provided the Chinese believers with rope cutters and they quickly got to work. Once the ropes were severed, they tore open the green plastic containers each holding forty-eight cardboard boxes of Bibles that were also sealed in plastic covers.

In keeping with the Chinese ways, the honey bees disappeared as quickly as they had come, carrying their Bibles in the traditional Chinese fashion – in two buckets with a sling across one shoulder. From my vantage point, it was an amazing sight to behold.

'There's thousands of them here,' came Brother David's voice crackling through the two-way radio from the beach. 'Keep the Bibles coming!'

About 5,000 Chinese Christians had arrived on Easter morning expecting the delivery, but the boat had not come on that occasion. Many of them must have wondered if we would let them down again. Despite that possibility and the great risk to themselves, the Scriptures were so desperately needed that they returned in even greater numbers on this night. We heard later that there were approximately 20,000 Chinese Christians on the scene for our delivery. Heavy brush lined the shore, giving cover to the multitude.

We were told of an elderly Christian lady who, for two years, had faithfully come each morning to this beach and prayed that God would send His Word to the Chinese Church. Her faithfulness was rewarded as God chose to answer her prayers in this miraculous way.

We had laid anchor at 9 p.m. expecting to be finished in a couple of hours. At 11 p.m. packages were still floating all around us with one Zodiac out of commission due to engine failure.

'You must leave now,' said an old Chinese fisherman who came on board the *Michael*. 'We can manage from here. The police could arrive at any moment. We've already seen informers on the beach.'

The Pearl of Great Price

Despite his warning, we pressed on until almost midnight. As the last packages slipped into the sea, the captain called out, 'Refloat the barge. We're waiting no longer.'

Other boats were arriving on the scene, curious to discover what we were up to. 'Please move them out of the way, Lord,' I cried. As I prayed, one by one, they began to turn and head out to sea.

'The pump motor won't start,' called out one of the crew.

'We'll leave as we are,' replied Captain Karl. 'Is everyone on board?'

When Captain Karl was satisfied that all the crew were accounted for, he shouted, 'Anchors away!'

Our engineer soon had the ship's engines pumping and we began to move. With the partially-submerged barge heavily listing to port, we lumbered back out to sea.

The water along the shore was full of dozens of packages. We prayed earnestly for the Chinese believers, wondering if they would have time to complete the task before the police arrived.

As we pulled away, one of the crew members who had been on shore said, 'That was truly amazing! They were not sure that we would come, but they told us that as they looked out to sea, they saw a vision of the Lord standing on the water and knew that He was awaiting our arrival. We had laid anchor exactly where He stood,' he said.

With the miracle landing completed, we headed for the safety of the twelve-mile limit where we were able to start the pump motors and re-float the barge.

'Where's the cake you brought, Eddie?' asked Brother David, smiling.

'Hang on, I'll go and get it,' I said.

When Betty knew for sure that I would be going on this trip, she had said, 'I would like to bake a celebration cake that you can eat once your task is completed.' She had made a rich fruitcake and had asked a friend of ours, Gwen Oram, an expert cake decorator, if she would add the icing.

'What would you like on it?' Gwen asked.

'We must be careful with the wording in case it is discovered by the Chinese,' said Betty. 'Their mission is called Project Pearl, so if you could, please decorate it with a pearl and the words, 'He has done all things well'.'

Gwen lovingly obliged. Those of us who could, gathered around in the galley. I thanked God for His mercy. He truly had done ALL THINGS WELL! Then we 'massacred' the cake. There were no ladies with a delicate hand to cut it so each of us sliced off a wedge according to our appetite.

With all of the crew safe and the barge floating high, we set our course for Paradise Bay, a beautiful cove in the Philippines across the South China Sea.

I was lying on my bunk when my thoughts went back to something God had shown me in a vision on the previous night.

I had seen three green lemons sitting around a table, and one after the other went up into the air and hovered around. They were bitter which meant that they must have been an enemy. They flew around, so I deduced that they must have been aircraft.

I told Brother David what I had seen and after a time of prayer together, we went out onto the darkened deck. Within a few moments, an aeroplane flew very low over us, its powerful lights trained on us.

'There goes our first lemon, brother,' I said. It was obviously a reconnaissance aircraft. There's two more yet to come.'

Within twenty minutes, another passed overhead. 'Are you waiting for the third one?' I asked my American friend. Shortly afterwards, the third came over us.

I wondered if there would be retaliation from what were obviously Chinese planes, but my vision hadn't shown any so I tried

The Pearl of Great Price

to get some sleep. Before finding any deep rest, dawn was upon us. When I went up on deck, the sun was completely obscured. The skies had covered and we were more hidden than we had been throughout trip. This would make it difficult for anyone to follow our activities.

I was looking forward to returning home. I recalled a Chinese leader saying, 'If you complete this task, it will be as great a miracle as Moses crossing the Red Sea.' She also said it would be one of the greatest works of God in her country.

We had, indeed, crossed the Red Sea of China. As I stood there thinking back, the ship's nose scything its way through the increasingly heavy waters, I asked myself what had motivated me to take on such a dangerous task.

LOVE was the only answer I could come up with. I had prayed so long and hard for China and on a number of occasions had even delivered suitcases full of Bibles to Christians there.

One Chinese Christian leader said, 'The Bibles you bring are like water on a desert sand.' In other words, they would disappear quickly.

The same could be said for the one million Bibles we had just delivered. It was just a drop in a bucket when compared to the great need of the multitudes of people in this mighty nation.

We had not planned to aggravate the Chinese authorities or insult its leaders. We had simply responded to the cries of the believers requesting that we bring 'food for our hungry lambs'.

God had safely taken us in and brought us out undetected by the defences of China. We had not come to install democracy or capitalism, but to bring them the Word of God and the blessing that the Word brings in its wake. Here was a quarter of the earth's population who had so few Bibles. Many Scriptures had been destroyed in the so-called Cultural Revolution so their need for Bibles had become desperate. That was the reason for Project Pearl.

The boat started to roll drunkenly. 'There's a storm ahead,' announced Captain Karl.

I made my way to the wheel house. It was my shift to keep the *Michael* on course. 'Keep your back firm against this pole,' said the previous helmsman as I gripped the wheel. 'If you don't hang on you'll be thrown out of the door.'

I quickly understood what he meant. The ship rolled and tossed, leaning perilously into the waves. I gripped the wheel tighter than ever, knowing that if I let go I would be tossed straight into the angry, churning sea.

We didn't know at the time, but this wrenching experience was to be our lot for the next three days.

It was almost impossible to chart our course as the swirling waters fought the wheel.

Brother David lay spread-eagled beside me on the floor. A chair rolled back and forth over the top of him. After so many hours, we became 'one' with the storm. The seas raged so fiercely that we often lost sight of the barge. Many of the crew were so sick that they could not leave their bunks. The cook had long since abandoned the galley since so few wanted to eat. Those who could, attended to themselves.

Johnny, from Australia, was suffering from dehydration. The constant sea-sickness and vomiting had taken such a toll that he could not lift his head off his pillow. His face was grey, and his eyes were rimmed in red and black from lack of sleep. He was so ill I wondered if he would make it home. I would take water to him and say, 'Johnny, swallow this,' then lift his head while he tried desperately to summon up the strength to swallow it.

For four days, I didn't eat or drink anything. I was just trying to hold on and felt that if I put anything in my stomach, that would be it. Thankfully, I was still able to take on my duties in the wheelhouse.

One midnight with the monsoon rain pounding down on us like sheets of metal, I tried to return to my cabin from the wheelhouse. I had just come down the ladder and reached the bottom deck when the sea violently surged across the ship, rolling it onto its side and dragging me with it. The water's force was so powerful that I felt like a fly on the wall, being sprayed with a high-pressure hose.

There and then, I could have been taken to a watery grave and no one would have missed me until morning. Somehow, I managed to cling to the ladder and await my chance to run to the cabin door and shut it quickly behind me. I was shaken to the bone.

My cabin had no ventilation and the air was getting too thick to breathe. I decided to try and sleep in the kitchen since it wasn't being used for anything else.

I took my mattress and put it under a table. Water was lapping into the room, swishing back and forth over me as I clung to the table leg, but I was too exhausted to care. I so desperately needed sleep that even this tropical nightmare could not keep me awake.

We were still rocking and rolling in the morning. At 8 a.m., soaked to the skin, I was back on duty. The captain was busying himself with the charts.

'Will we reach port by the twenty-third, Karl?' I asked him.

'No,' was his instant reply. 'We're only moving at two knots.'

'But, we have to be there by then,' I said. 'It's my Silver Wedding anniversary and I'm supposed to be home for the celebration. Betty doesn't even know whether I'm dead or alive.'

'I'm sorry, but there's nothing we can do about it,' he said matter-of-factly.

On the following day, the storm began to abate. The seas were still turbulent, but they were beginning to settle down. This enabled the captain to increase our speed.

My continual prayer was, 'Lord, please let me call Betty in time for our wedding anniversary.'

My spirits began to rise when one of the crew shouted out through cupped hands, 'Land ahoy.' It was the first signal that we were approaching the northern tip of the Philippines.

I went on deck with Brother David and we watched the foam-streaked water narrow between us and the shore. We were close to Subic Bay, an American naval base, when we heard the deafening noise of a jet plane roaring overhead.

'Look at that,' said Brother David pointing skyward, 'they're giving a victory roll. I bet they've been watching us by satellite the whole time.'

(At a later date, when Betty and I were visiting Washington DC, we met with a White House official who had been part of a group in Washington that had been praying for the success of Project Pearl. It seemed quite clear to me by what he said, that we had, indeed, been monitored from 'above' during the whole time.)

As we neared port, it was the twenty-third of June. *Will we make it?* I wondered. *What is the difference in time between New Zealand and the Philippines?*

A number of whales with their young calves had accompanied us down the coast and continued to escort us into the harbour. I had never before seen a sight as beautiful as the calves rising up on their mother's backs, then slipping back into the water as they majestically slid through the ocean alongside the ship. They were no more than twenty feet away from us.

As soon as we dropped anchor in Paradise Bay, I told Captain Karl, 'I'm heading for the shore.'

'Oh no you're not!' he said firmly. 'We've got to go through customs first.'

I was anxious. *I wish they'd hurry,* I thought.

While the Filipino customs officials went through the formalities, I prepared for shore. My trousers had become shorts when I removed the legs with a sharp knife during the storm. They were laden with salt. They were worn and filthy. I kicked them off and threw them over the side. They had served their purpose.

I wanted to be ready as soon as we were allowed to get off the ship. I was about to become a landlubber again! I couldn't afford to lose a moment. Time was running out.

We finally got our clearance. Brother David could see how anxious I was to talk to Betty so he escorted me to the nearest phone.

I dialed my home number and waited as the phone rang and rang. *Am I in time?* I wondered as doubt filled my mind. My heart was thudding heavily.

'Hello.' Betty's voice sounded so beautiful.

'Sweetheart,' I whispered excitedly, 'happy wedding anniversary.'

'You made it!' Her voice cracked with emotion. 'Praise the Lord, you've made it' She began to shed a few tears.

It was 10:15 p.m. New Zealand time.

'Family and friends have been in to celebrate,' she informed me. 'They've only just left. We didn't know whether you were alive or not!'

It had been three weeks since I had contacted her. A lump came into my throat as I spoke to my bride from across the many miles. Against all odds, I had reached Betty on our special day.

The giant Bible delivery was over and it had been a great success. As a result, believers in China would never be the same.

For them, it was a 'Pearl of Great Price'.

Chapter Thirteen

In the Air to Mandalay

I gasped for breath in the sauna-like heat that enveloped me as I walked across the melting tarmac at Rangoon (now Yangon) Airport to board a plane for Mandalay. Noticing two fire extinguishers standing on a trolly beside the ramshackle Fokker Friendship aircraft that Betty and I were about to board, I stopped in my tracks.

'Excuse me sir,' I asked the uniformed man standing guard over them. 'What are they for?' He smiled knowingly. 'One of the engines caught fire yesterday, sir,' he said. 'These are here in case it happens again.'

I looked at him and then at the aeroplane in disbelief. Then I saw that the plane's tyres had absolutely no tread on them and they had even worn through to the canvas in several places.

'We're not really flying in this old crate, are we?' asked Betty incredulously. Even under good circumstances, flying was a nightmare for her. But this was ridiculous.

'We've flown in the old things before, honey,' I said, trying to comfort her. 'The Lord will carry us, as He always has.'

Betty and I climbed the steep stairs into the worn, old plane and took our seats. Almost immediately, the engines started to roar and our ancient transport rumbled to the end of the runway.

I happened to turn around and see the stewardess unsuccessfully trying to wrestle the door shut. She began kicking loose metal along the bottom of the door in hopes that would help.

'I'd better try and do something,' I thought, observing her plight. Desperately, I freed myself from the safety belt and hurried to her aid. Between the two of us we were able to force the stubborn door shut just in time for take-off.

I stumbled back to my seat and sat down, or I should say, *fell* down. As I landed, the back of my seat collapsed and landed in the lap of the passenger behind me. I apologised and tried to lift it back up. In doing so, I bumped the plastic window frame, breaking it loose, and ended up wearing it as a necklace.

In the midst of this comedy of errors, I hardly noticed that we were airborne.

Betty and I were passing through Burma (now known as Myanmar) with one of our tour groups from New Zealand. There were fourteen of us carrying a total of 700 Bibles plus Sunday School materials, many different kinds of toiletries, and other small gifts for Christians in Mandalay. My team had just come from China via Bangkok and we were now on our way to Burma. This is the largest country in Southeast Asia – approximately the same size as Texas and Connecticut combined. It was already proving to be an eventful trip.

As we reached travelling altitude, our pilot's voice came over the intercom and announced, 'Ladies and gentlemen, I apologise for any discomfort that you may be feeling. One of our starboard engines has cut out and we will not be able to operate the air conditioners.'

A shudder rattled through the plane as he added, 'Don't worry, we will be landing shortly at Rangoon.'

As we made our final approach, swooping low over water-soaked rice paddies, I wasn't thinking so much about the landing but about our upcoming encounter in the customs shed. After all, we had a huge consignment of Bibles (which we had chosen to call 'bread') with us. I anticipated that the Burmese wouldn't be too happy with having them casually carried into their country.

Memories of the previous trip to Burma that I had taken with thirteen other Kiwis, rushed into my mind. Just like before, it was stiflingly hot as we crossed the tarmac toward the terminal. The air was almost too heavy to breathe and its weight forced us to move in slow motion. Time seemed to come to a complete standstill. The terminal didn't appear to have changed since the British left this country in the late 1940s.

Packed like sardines into the customs area, we began to wilt from the clinging humidity. I directed my group to wait around the perimeter of the room while I dealt with the customs officials.

'Just wait until I call you,' I instructed them. A sense of excitement overtook me as I went to seek clearance for my team with the secret 'bread.' The Burmese customs officials were expecting our group and I knew from previous trips that I, as the leader, would be the only one needed to sort out the paperwork.

'Please sit here,' said the chief customs officer as he pushed his spectacles down his nose. He smiled a fake smile at me and motioned toward the pile of customs forms and passports that I had gathered from my group.

I handed them to him, and awaited his response. The extreme heat and humidity made it seem as though he took forever to study the mound of documents. Then he finally said, 'Call your people to collect their baggage and bring it for inspection.'

As our suitcases were opened one-by-one, a nearby woman officer announced loudly in English, 'These people have Bibles!'

The senior officer looked at me and asked sternly, 'Are your people carrying Bibles?'

'Yes, a few,' I replied, clammy perspiration formed on my palms as I tried very hard to appear relaxed. 'We have some for the churches, and for the Bible Society also.'

'Bible Society,' he said with a smile. 'That is good.'

He waved a hand of dismissal toward the woman officer who was hovering nearby awaiting his instructions and said something to her in Burmese. I don't know what it was, but as far as I was concerned, it meant, 'Don't worry, everything is all right.'

The man went back to inspecting our papers as the remainder of our bags were being checked. As I looked over this scene, the blood drained from my face.

While in Bangkok, I had advised the team to place all of their Bibles in the bottom of their suitcases underneath the other gifts and personal effects. That way, they would be more difficult to detect.

Jenny, a member of our team, lifted her newly-purchased suitcase onto the counter for inspection, not realising that she had placed it upside down. When her bag was opened, to our horror, there they were – Bibles … lots of them sitting neatly on top of everything, in plain view of Jenny, myself, the team, and that same female customs officer.

The officer immediately turned to the senior official. Closing her eyes and slapping a hand over her forehead, she exclaimed, 'They have more Bibles!' The senior officer seemed to be losing patience with the nearly hysterical woman, and he didn't even look up. With a gruff voice, he dismissed her once again.

'You may all go through,' he said with one eyebrow raised. We emerged from the terminal building and headed for the bus that would take us to our final flight to Mandalay. Near the bus, we were confronted by a pitiful collection of ragged children, their hands outstretched begging for anything that we might be able to give. We gave them the orchids that we had received while boarding the plane in Bangkok.

'Are you okay?' I asked Jenny.

'I am now,' she responded with a faint smile, 'but I sure got a fright.'

We were so grateful to God that none of the Scriptures were lost. We hadn't come to see the sights such as the Shwedagon Pagoda (the largest and oldest Buddhist temple in the world), but to work – to bless our Burmese brothers and sisters with the Word of God. If the Bibles had been confiscated in customs, the whole trip would have been a loss.

Our last trip through customs went much more smoothly and again, nothing was confiscated. Still with all that was happening with our aircraft, our group from New Zealand was feeling quite unnerved. Many of them had never travelled overseas before.

'Why are we flying so low?' asked one member of the team.

'I think the pilot's following the river,' I said jokingly.

Despite the unexplained aerobatics, we touched down safely in Mandalay, breathing deep sighs of relief as the landing gear came in contact with the ground.

As we gathered at the bottom of the stairs, we were greeted by a guide who said, 'We – all of us here – are in Mandalay.'

He said it as if he were solving a big mystery. We couldn't help but smile at his superfluous statement.

By the time we arrived at our hotel, everyone spoke in whispers from exhaustion. I suggested that they rest in the air-conditioned rooms. I planned to look for our contact – a pastor I met on my previous trip.

I soon found him and we set our plans for the delivery that night. I needed to arrange transportation for my fourteen-member team plus a quarter-of-a-ton of Bibles. We brooded over the problem until, eventually, my Burmese friend came upon an acceptable solution. All that was available, he explained, smiling apologetically, were donkey carts. By our calculations, we would need five of them. My contact and I agreed to rendezvous at 9 p.m.

The night was warm and still. Under a canopy of stars, we haggled with the donkey cart owners until the matter was satisfactorily settled. We went right to work, haunted by the fear of being caught. We quickly loaded people and 'bread' into the small carts. Some of the donkeys seemed far too small for the task ahead, but we had no alternative.

I placed Joyce, a lady larger than the Burmese, into a cart and threw three bags of Bibles in behind her. Another member of our team jumped on board, and I (also rather robust) climbed on the back. Our little donkey suddenly became airborne, dangling helplessly from the shafts. Our weight had lifted him completely off the ground. We quickly dismounted and removed some of the bags so that the poor animal could return to terra firma.

Clip, clop, clip, clop went our convoy as we headed through the darkened streets penetrating the decaying slums of Mandalay with only a candlelight on each side of our carts to illuminate our way. Despite the nervousness that accompanied us on our secret mission, we all enjoyed the horse and carriage experience which felt like a trip backwards in time.

After twenty minutes, we arrived at our destination – a church on the outskirts of the former capital city of Burma.

'Watch out for the snakes!' our contact cried. Everyone shuddered, then cautiously walked with short, uneven steps along the centre of the narrow path that led to our pre-arranged 'drop' point. Lugging our bags full of 'bread', we carefully bumped our way toward a clump of trees where the small church was, each of us listening for the rustle of snakes moving through the dry underbrush. Dense, tropical air magnified every sound. I jumped as a dead twig snapped underfoot.

'Thank you for coming,' said Pastor Michael who emerged from the thatch-roofed sanctuary to greet us. He warmly shook hands with each member of our group.

'We have many Bibles,' I told the young pastor. 'Where would you like us to put them?'

'Place them all on top of the table by the pulpit,' he said directly.

'Are you sure this won't get you into trouble?' I asked. 'We have so many.' The church was quickly filling with members of his congregation, and I was afraid that a public display of so much 'bread' might attract too much attention and get the pastor into trouble.

'No, it will be a great encouragement to the people,' he said.

We emptied our bags and were invited to sit in the front, facing the congregation of Burmese believers. They were a colourful group. The men and the women all wore long multi-coloured 'skirts' called longyi. In such a hot climate, they helped to keep them cool.

They welcomed us with a song and asked us to reciprocate. I led our group in a rendition of 'Power in the Blood'. Then the children sang some choruses.

'Would you bring us a word, Brother Eddie,' the pastor requested. I stood and said, 'Yes, pastor. I would love to.

But first, would you mind if we gave some of these Bibles to those in your congregation who don't own one.'

He gave the invitation, and I was amazed when almost all of the one hundred people there came forward. I had only been expecting a few. They pressed in around us for the Word of God, and I was reminded of the passage of Scripture in Luke 5 where a multitude had done the same to Jesus. Such was the hunger and need of these people for the Word of God, but not just for themselves. They also begged for copies for their relatives and neighbours.

There were several present who had bad eyesight – some for many years. Before leaving New Zealand, we had asked people to donate their spare eye-glasses for us to deliver to our needy Burmese brethren. The response was overwhelming, and it was a great joy to see the excitement of some of these people as they were able to read again after so long. Somehow (not really so mysteriously), the donated glasses matched perfectly the visual needs of our new friends. Another miracle orchestrated by our Lord.

I shared with them from Matthew 8 how Jesus had touched the leper and healed him. 'This story shows that His touch can cleanse us sinners.' I told them that we all need cleansing from sin.

I told them of the centurion who met Jesus, and how his display of faith brought healing to his servant.

I went on to cite the story of Peter's mother-in-law who was sick with a raging fever. 'Jesus touched her hand and she rose up and served,' I said. 'This touch of the Lord was given as power for service. He healed her, empowering her to serve them.'

'Without faith it is impossible to please God, and faith brings healing,' I said. 'As is your faith, so be it to you.'

I explained that the touch of the Spirit of God is still needed today for our ministries to be successful, and that we all need *To Catch the Wind*, if we are to be mightily used by the Lord.

'Thank you for bringing this to me,' said Timothy, a tiny Burmese evangelist, as he lovingly handled the loudspeaker I gave him. On our last trip, he had asked if we could possibly bring one. The Lord used us to answer his request.

'I often speak in the open-air and this will be a great help to reach the large crowds,' he explained.

As Timothy and I stood in the shadows close to our hotel, I asked him, 'Are there any Christians in the city of Pagan? I've heard that there are only Buddhist temples there.'

Excitedly, he responded, 'We've just finished an outreach there and five families came to the Lord, but they don't yet have any Bibles.'

I gave Timothy the few remaining Bibles and enough money to

pay his fare to Pagan to deliver the Bibles and encourage the new believers.

'Please don't forget us when you get home,' he said sincerely. 'It is such an encouragement to know we are not forgotten.'

Earlier that day, Timothy had taken me to his little grass-topped prayer house where a dozen or so believers gathered regularly for intercession.

As we stood together ready to part, he solemnly promised, 'Brother Eddie, we will always pray for you in our prayer house that God will bless your work.'

Soon, he had moved off into the shadows. We waved until he was completely out of sight.

'What precious people these are,' I remarked to one of my group. 'We must come again soon, and bring them more help.' The believers of this forgotten nation had won a special place in my heart.

Chapter Fourteen

Revelations on the Ho Chi Minh Trail

'I've made arrangements for our Bible delivery to start at 7 p.m.,' I told my group. We had just come from Bangkok to Tan Son Bhut Airport in Ho Chi Minh City. This city was named in honour of Vietnam's deceased independence leader – many of us still remember it as Saigon, however.

As Yvonne and Gregg, my daughter and son, and I gazed out the window of the aeroplane during our descent, I pointed out the old bunkers where US fighter jets had been stored during the war. I explained to them that on April 30, 1975, Hanoi forces 'liberated' Saigon.

'This land has suffered tremendously,' I added. 'They've seen nothing but war for several decades. Our plan now is to mend the wounds with The Word.'

This was my second trip to Vietnam, but I was feeling a bit apprehensive. It was my eldest daughter's first time through a communist border. Greg had been to China and to Burma with me.

'It could be a tough search,' I told Yvonne. 'Don't worry, I'll be keeping my eye on you, dear. Just keep your heart open to the Lord. He will be our deliverer.'

Most of the people in our group were nervous about attempting to clear customs with the large number of Bibles that we carried, so

I walked among them and encouraged them by declaring, 'The Lord is with us, and His heart is to see this 'bread' delivered to Vietnam.'

I watched closely as Yvonne faced a woman customs official. Her suitcase, like all of them, was full of Vietnamese Bibles. The officer wasn't as hard-faced or suspicious as some of the others, and after a few formalities she waved Yvonne through the gate. My daughter cast a wry smile in my direction, and I felt a great load lift from my shoulders as I saw her disappear through the gate.

We noticed that other visitors were experiencing problems but thank God, we had found favour with the customs officers. Only two of our suitcases were opened and no Bibles were detected.

'Meet me in my room in one hour,' I told our group after we had completed our hotel registration. 'We need to be careful,' I told them, 'we don't want to bring problems to our brothers and sisters. When we leave the hotel, we will need to go in small groups so as not to attract attention. Each of you bring only a third of your load.'

I studied my watch. It was five minutes to seven. 'Let's hit it!' I told Daniel, my roommate. We picked up our bags and headed for the stairs. Our group had been divided into rooms on three separate floors. Daniel and I were on the sixth floor. We went down one floor only to find that some of the others were waiting for us. They slammed their doors and followed like copycats. We went down to the next floor, and the same thing happened.

So here we were, all entering the foyer at the same time, and each of us had shoulder bags packed with Bibles. *We MUST look conspicuous,* I thought. *This is just what I didn't want to happen.*

I could see that we had become the centre of attention. Hotel attendants appeared agitated and began yelling out in Vietnamese. It seemed they wanted someone to tell them what to do.

'Go, go,' I hissed, hurrying my team out the front doors. 'Follow me.'

I led them across the darkened street to two waiting vehicles that I had previously arranged. We were observed only by a soup vendor. As we drove off, our drivers had to take evasive action to avoid becoming tangled in a mess of bicycle taxis that were vying for business around the hotel. It did not appear that we had been followed, and we all arrived safely at our delivery point – a house in the suburbs.

As we climbed from the vehicles, we were surrounded by a group of smiling Vietnamese Christians. 'This way,' said one of the men. 'We have many people waiting for you upstairs.'

We were welcomed by several house church leaders, then each of us was handed a glass of Coca-Cola, a welcome thirst-quencher in this tropical climate. Well-greeted and refreshed, we began our meeting as the Bibles were being unloaded from the vehicles and whisked away. I discovered that many of Ho Chi Minh City's 3.5 million people live in fear of the security police and a well-organised network of government informers. These believers did not live in fear, however, but in wisdom. Still, they were careful not to draw attention to their activities.

As usual, the men asked if I would 'bring the Word'. They hung on every word that I shared from the Holy Scriptures. I wished that those in my own country were as hungry to hear the precious Word of God as these oppressed brethren.

That night, at the conclusion of the service, there were several who committed their lives to the Lord. After the altar call, I began to pray for the house church leaders. As I stood before them, I felt the Spirit of God giving me a message for each of them.

As I spoke these messages audibly, individual heads would nod, and I knew that the words were accurate and encouraging.

I remained until the early hours of the morning, ministering to the group of leaders. One of the men had recorded all that I said and the following day, I was told that they had stayed up all night writing down each message the Lord had given them through me.

We made plans for our next Bible delivery. It was to be at 2 p.m. the following day. Arrangements were made for vehicles to pick us up in different parts of the city. We didn't want observers to figure out what we were doing.

'You are free to go shopping for the morning, but let's all meet back in my room at one o'clock sharp. Don't bring your 'bread' with you,' I told the group over breakfast. 'Extra security has been put on my floor. Take care!'

I noticed three Vietnamese men had checked into rooms opposite mine and always left their doors ajar. Every time I opened my door, they came and stood at theirs. The team arrived in ones and twos and behind closed doors, we began a low-key prayer meeting for the safe delivery of our life-changing load.

While we prayed, a vision appeared to me showing a large piece of fruit. I thanked the Lord that this was going to be a fruitful operation. But then, I saw that the piece of fruit was being consumed by a multitude of worms and was soon gone.

'It's *not* time to move,' I said as I related the vision. 'We will lose everything if we go now.'

For the sake of our Vietnamese friends, I had been apprehensive of a daytime pick-up. If they were caught cooperating with us on our mission, their penalties would be severe, but they pressed me, saying that 'time is of the essence.'

Now I had to contact them and make other arrangements. Not wanting to use the hotel telephone, I left the building, and found a phone in a nearby shop.

'Can I use your phone?' I asked the man who was half asleep behind the counter. He looked at me vacantly, so I pointed to the ancient telephone. I was feeling more tense than usual because of the close call we'd had the previous evening due to our own bumbling.

The man gently nodded his head as if to say, 'Be my guest.' I changed the delivery arrangements to seven o'clock that evening. I had mixed feelings about this because that was the same time we had left the night before. Surely they would be watching for us again.

Just prior to dinner, we gathered in Yvonne's room and I told the others of the new plans.

'This time, let's not all arrive in the lobby together! It would be good if some of us could go outside early and do a little 'window shopping.' Please watch closely for our vehicles,' I instructed.

During dinner, a commotion broke out in the reception area, then the hotel staff began shouting and ran out into the street.

'What's happening?' I asked the waiter, wondering if we had caused the problem. My mind began to race. I imagined that possibly the police had arrived and were about to make a search of our rooms.

'There's a fire down the road,' said the waiter.

'Is it in the hotel?' I queried.

'No, it's a few buildings away,' With that, he raced off to observe the blaze.

'Let's go and see what's happening out there,' I told the team. We joined the jostling, chattering crowd that had flocked to the towering inferno. A fourteen-storey building was completely ablaze. The sky lit up as the flames leaped out of windows and raced from storey to storey. I moved closer to watch several fire engines that had arrived on the scene. Their water hoses were not carrying enough pressure even to start dampening down the fire. The blaze was totally out of control and threatened to engulf the entire block of buildings – including our hotel.

I looked at my watch. We were just minutes away from our rendezvous time. 'Come on!' I called above the noise of the burgeoning crowd. 'We have a job to do!'

We hurried back to the hotel and loaded our bags with the

Vietnamese Scriptures. There wasn't a soul to be seen in the reception area. They were all watching the burning building.

Our drivers hardly noticed us as they stood among the enthralled crowd, watching the disaster. We loaded our bags into the transport and joined them, gazing in awe as the powerful flames devoured the tall structure. What was a tragedy for others, had become a blessing for us. For whatever reason God had allowed this disaster, it had become a more than suitable cover for us.

We eventually left the fire scene with our Vietnamese drivers, to spend some wonderful time in fellowship with a new group of believers. When we returned about four hours later, the fire had not yet reached the top of the building.

'Was anybody killed,' I asked some of the onlookers.

'Yes' was the answer of some, while others said, 'No.'

I later discovered that those responsible for the security of the building had been arrested.

'Could you come and speak to our people tomorrow,' the local pastor asked me. 'I will arrange an all-day meeting with leaders from many churches, if you will come.'

I had already spent twelve hours that day preaching and ministering to Vietnamese brethren, but their hunger for the Word was insatiable.

'I will be happy to come and bring the rest of the group with me,' I said, my voice hoarse and cracking. 'I'm sure many of them would also like to share with you the things that God has done in *their* lives.'

Our group included believers from Australia and New Zealand. We had expanded Mission Outreach and were involved in recruiting couriers from Australia as well as from New Zealand.

'I would like to hire a boat for the day,' said the pastor, 'but it would be very costly.'

'How much?' I asked him.

'About US $150,' he said.

'If you think it's a good idea, I'll be happy to pay,' I said. His face lit up with joy.

'I will do it. I'll arrange for you to be picked up in the morning,' he said.

True to his word, we were picked up, then driven through an ocean of traffic as bicycle and pedicab (bicycle-powered rickshaws) bells clanged, and motor-bike horns sounded. In two hours, we were out of the city and at the edge of the Mekong River.

'That's a fine looking boat,' I observed. 'How many people will it carry?'

'Perhaps two-hundred,' our contact replied.

There was already a good number of people on board when we came across the ramp onto the deck. It wasn't long before the engines began to thump, and we were off.

As the boat slipped away from the riverbank, the Vietnamese believers began strumming their guitars and singing 'This is the day that the Lord has made.' Their beautiful voices echoed across the river.

'What a friend we have in Jesus' came next. I was touched by the fact that their hymns of praise were the same that we sang in the West.

The singing continued for an hour. It was a joy to be with these people. I thought of the irony of sailing on a river that had seen so much war, and yet these believers were singing praises to the Prince of Peace.

When the music stopped, several of the leaders warmly welcomed us, and I responded in kind to their good wishes. Each member of our team gave a testimony of their faith in God. When it was time for the sermon, I opened the Scriptures and spoke to my floating congregation about Gideon.

'This man with his small group of people, released the nation of Israel from the clutches of the Midianites,' I observed. 'God does not need large numbers to set His people free, He just needs committed, obedient people prepared to respond to His voice.'

I told them of the three articles that Gideon took with him into battle. One was the trumpet which represented proclaiming the Word of the Lord. The second was the clay vessel which spoke of our flesh and the third was the torch which represented the Holy Spirit.

'Gideon's followers were to break the clay vessels,' I continued. 'To gain our victory, we must eliminate the flesh. Gideon sounded the trumpet. With the sounding of the trumpet came the torches, bringing great confusion to the enemy who began to destroy each other. We, too, must 'sound' the Word of the Lord into the camp of the enemy.

'It is the wind of the Holy Spirit that is the key to all of God's great works. Let us acknowledge this precious third person of the Godhead and invite Him in to all our endeavours.'

I asked those who had not received the release of the Holy Spirit in their lives to come forward. Large numbers came and as they did, I felt a wind blowing against my left arm. It was an unusual feeling, so I looked out at the trees on the riverbank to see if they were moving, but they were completely still.

As I turned to face the group, the wind of the Holy Spirit suddenly swept over them as at Pentecost and they began to speak in tongues.

Rudy and Kay Bruns, the directors of Mission Outreach Australia, were present on that day. Rudy had walked toward the group to see what was happening and said, 'Lord, if you want me to speak in tongues, then let it be!'

Immediately, he too caught the wind of the Holy Spirit and began speaking in a heavenly language. Kay was overjoyed since she had longed for many years that Rudy would share this edifying, and glorious experience. For Rudy, as for these wonderful Vietnamese believers, this was a day *To Catch the Wind* of the Holy Spirit in a new and powerful way.

'Welcome to the killing fields,' said our smiling guide shortly after we entered Phnom Penh, the capital of Cambodia. It seemed paradoxical for him to make such a statement with a broad smile on his face. That smile, I soon discovered, was one of politeness, not of joy.

The guide continued, 'This is the land where the genocidal dictator, Pol Pot, tried to set the clock back 4,000 years. In the process, he killed as many as three million of my countrymen.'

My little group stood shocked into silence, trying to take in the enormity of what our guide had just said. We were baking in the 90 degree temperature with the humidity running at around 80 per cent, but it was the horror of what we heard, not the clammy heat, that caused us to sweat.

We had hired a bus in Ho Chi Minh City to make the ten-hour journey to this tragic, forgotten land.

'The risks are high,' the travel agent had warned. 'There are frequently shootings on the road between here and Phnom Penh, and bandits sometimes hold up buses, robbing the travellers. But if you insist, you can try and make it.'

I shared these possible dangers with my team, but they all agreed that it was vital that we make the trip. Our aim was to seek information on the church in Cambodia, and also to try to experience a little of their pain.

Our driver kept his foot pressed to the floor as we shot along historic Route 1 which had functioned as an incursion route for the South Vietnamese army during the Vietnam War. It led into Cambodia's 'Parrot's Beak.' Although the two cities are less than 200 miles apart, the drive seemed to take forever.

Our driver gave no signals when he pulled out to pass foul-smelling tractors, braces of oxen, or Soviet-made trucks laden with melons or foam-rubber mattresses. We flew across bridges and through populated areas at rocket speed, sending terrified chickens flying in all directions.

When the Vietnamese withdrew their estimated 170,000 troops from Cambodia, they had erected an enormous wooden victory arch at the border which still marks the frontier. After presenting two copies of our customs and passport control declarations, we crossed the border into the 'killing fields.'

The heavy traffic of Vietnam evaporated as we moved into Cambodia. We gazed out of the window of our bus as the landscape alternated between flooded rice paddies and war-ravaged towns whose shops had been burned out shells for fifteen years.

We were soon approaching Phnom Penh, still on Route 1 which turned out to be one of only two roads in the country that remained paved.

The city itself, like the rest of Cambodia, was devastated by the war. Potholes littered the highway and our driver had to swerve constantly to avoid them.

On arrival we were taken to the Cambodiana Hotel, the largest building in the country, and attractive. It is a five-storey structure laid out along the Mekong River in a manner meant to resemble a Cambodian pagoda. Despite the refreshing the hotel afforded us, our visit to the 'killing fields' proved horrendous. We stood paralysed as our guide pointed out a monument with shelves which contained more than 20,000 skulls.

'Many of these are the skulls of innocent children,' he explained.

'I escaped from this camp and was put out on a farm to work. Even out there, many children and young people were killed, their bodies left lying in the fields to be picked clean by wild animals and vultures.

'In front of their mothers, Pol Pot's henchmen would take hold of a child and tear him limb from limb. They would throw them into mass graves. About 250 bodies were buried in each hole after they had been stripped of their clothing.'

He told us that many of the adults were bludgeoned to death by rifle butts and garden hoes. Those that had not died immediately suffered an agonising death by being buried alive in the mass graves. The guide took us to see some of Pol Pot's torture chambers and many in our group could not cope with the heinous pictures displayed there.

'Millions of my people were either killed or brutally displaced from their homes during the terrifying years of the Khmer Rouge led by Pol Pot,' he explained. 'Some estimate that nearly half the population perished during this man's reign of terror.'

Once the tour was over, most felt that they had seen enough of this ghastly tragedy, so they hired transportation to see more of the city. Phnom Penh was a virtual ghost-town in Pol Pot's day.

Today it supports a population of 700,000. Some of our group discovered that rush hours were back in vogue with bicycles, three-wheeled rickshaws, and Japanese-made motorcycles jockeying for space in the dusty streets. In the many once shuttered stores, dry-goods merchants, welding shops and repair shops had reopened.

In the open-air market they saw everything from Nescafe to Sears jogging shoes and Sharp stereos on sale – all smuggled in by Thai fishing boats. As our people bought things, they could not shake an overwhelming feeling of compassion for this nation that had seen so many perish – and for what?

Cambodia still bears deep scars. Countless deserted towns dot the landscape and many believe that Phnom Penh is Asia's filthiest capital. Its streets were flooded with raw sewage leaking from broken pipes, mixing a nauseating stench with the already-polluted air. The grey-streaked buildings were broken down.

Jacob (one of the team) and I had been given addresses of believers, and our heart's desire was to find them and discover how they were. We knew that during the terrible years of Pol Pot, all religious activities had been forbidden. Christian leaders were killed. Even the mosques and Buddhist temples were looted and destroyed.

We hired a bicycle-taxi and our 'driver' was able to pinpoint the address for us. We discovered that this particular contact was in an old building which had been converted into a church. We climbed two flights of rickety steps. When we reached the top, I pushed open a door and looked inside a room where a group of people were sitting on handmade pews. We were met with startled looks. This was part of Cambodia's spiritual underground, the equivalent of the catacombs where early Christians hid their faith from the Romans.

'Yes, can I help you?' said a middle-aged man in excellent English. He came toward us in this attic church.

I explained that we would like to learn more about the Cambodian church. With excitement in his voice, he said there were the beginning signs of a real revival in the land.

'In the last few months, our church has gone from a few members to over two hundred,' he said. 'About ten churches and house churches have now been established in this city.'

I asked him if there was religious freedom in the land.

'No,' he said, 'except in four states. Even there, the Buddhists are very uncomfortable with any Christian presence. Out of four million people living in our country, only a few are believers.'

'What are your needs?' I asked.

'Bible study materials,' said our newfound friend. 'All our leaders have been killed or have left the country, and we have no Bible schools here. Children are a priority for us, too, but we also have no Sunday School equipment.'

He paused for a moment, then said with a deep yearning in his voice, 'Above everything else, we need Bibles.'

I had brought a few English Bibles and a selection of Cambodian-language Gospels, and gave them to him.

'Thank you dear brother,' said our Cambodian friend as he held a Bible close to his heart. With tears brimming, he added urgently, 'Whatever *can* be done, should be done *now!*'

I gave an invitation for a group of Cambodian leaders to come to my hotel room that night. I called my team together to meet them. As my group heard the heart-rending testimonies of these men – many of them had lost loved ones in the Cambodian holocaust – I could sense a softening of their hearts.

One by one, our team members went to a Cambodian and hugged him tight. Words could not express what they felt at that moment.

I finally rose to my feet to address all who had gathered with us.

'I must tell you that you, the leaders of the Christian church in Cambodia, must come against the Goddess of Death, the idol that has been worshipped by your nation for centuries,' I said with conviction.

'Through believing prayer, you must break its power and release life upon your people. You also have to bind the wicked Pol Pot, murderer of your people and ask God to remove him and replace him with righteous leaders.'

I stated that we should not wait, but we needed to pray then and there against this idol.

'We must then release the precious influence of the Spirit of God upon the nation,' I said.

These Cambodian Christians joined together in prayer. After a powerful time of intercession, one of them stood up and declared, 'We will take this message to the rest of the believers. We believe this is a message from God that they need to hear and take action.'

I asked my team to empty their bags and present the group with the Bibles and Gospel tracts that they had carried in. After a great time of fellowship, our friends eventually left, many burdens having been lifted from their shoulders. They loaded down their motorbikes with the precious cargo that we had given them, and headed off to beat the 10 p.m. curfew.

This had been a difficult journey for all of us. We had entered a new battlefield and done spiritual warfare against the tremendous powers of darkness in Cambodia. I felt certain, however, that we had won a victory over Satan and we could believe that the spirit of death would no longer hover over the 'killing fields.'

Chapter Fifteen

The Roof of the World

'I'm going to push for a visit to Tibet, honey,' I told Betty as we stood gazing out of our lounge window. Tendrils of mist as white and fine as lace floated past. They partly obscured our view of Mount Maunganui about five miles away. Green fields spotted with sheep and goats, provided a beautiful foreground for this near picture-perfect landscape.

I had long been intrigued by the strange land that had been invaded by the Chinese communists in 1951. In studying Tibet's history, I learned that during an uprising in 1959, the country's religious leader (the Dalai Lama) had fled to India. The communists were able to break the Buddhist traditions of Tibet which had really only survived in the ceremonies of a handful of refugees. There had been some signs of revival in the 1980s, but I had no idea if there were any Christians at all in this mountainous nation. Some reports in the West said that there were none at all, but I wanted to discover the truth for myself. Tibet covers 2.5 million square kilometres at an average height of 4,500 metres – hence its nickname, 'The Roof of the World.'

Three years before, a vision had drawn my attention to this forgotten land. It happened while I was in Nepal, the monarchical Hindu state between India and Tibet. I was there, attempting to get into Tibet. Sadly, the doors were closed tighter than a drum.

Constant uprisings were taking place by the Tibetans against the Chinese 'invaders' and while I was in Nepal, the border had again been closed to foreigners.

I was staying in a Kathmandu hotel when the vision appeared to me during a time of prayer. I 'saw' the top of Mount Everest with three thrones placed on top of its soaring peaks. One throne was white, a second was grey, and the third was black. In this vision, Satan walked to and fro across the mountain with his arms outstretched, looking like a bat.

After seeing this astonishing sight, I asked my Nepalese guide what a bat indicated to him as a Hindu.

'Excessive sin,' was his frank reply.

The Holy Spirit revealed the meaning of what I had just seen to me. The white throne represented deception. Satan was an angel of light whose aim was to deceive the nations. The grey represented humanism. Buddha had been born at the foot of Mount Everest, and Buddhism states that everything stems from the mind of man himself. The black throne represented Satan's current work in leading the nations into excessive sin.

I read in Isaiah 14:12-14, *'How art thou fallen from heaven, O Lucifer, son of the morning! How art thou cut down to the ground, who didst weaken the nations! … I will exalt my throne above the stars of God; I will sit also upon the mount of the congregation, in the sides of the north, I will ascend above the heights of the clouds, I will be like the most High.'*

I had always pictured Satan as the prince of the power of the air, floating around somewhere up there, but in reality, I realised he was probably sitting on top of the earth.

If this were true, Tibet was where his seat could be. I believed God wanted me to go and 'do spiritual battle' with him there. My understanding was that God wanted to match His own people who were full of the Holy Spirit against Satan. In Luke 10:19, Jesus said,

'Behold I give unto you power [authority] to tread on serpents and scorpions, and over all the power of the enemy…'

Even though I could not enter Tibet on that first occasion, my heart was set on penetrating this uniquely beautiful, unusual land. Betty was concerned that we didn't appear to be making any headway in following through with a Tibetan trip although the vision had taken place years before.

'How long has it been since we began the search for those Tibetan Bibles?' she asked me one day.

'It must be at least eighteen months since I was last in touch with the Bible Society,' I replied. 'At that time they were not sure whether they had any or not, and they were going to make inquiries through other offices around the world to see if any could be found. They haven't been back in touch, but I feel that it's time to go to Tibet,' I said.

It was Monday night when a group of nine people gathered in our Mission Outreach office. As I looked around the room, I had to smile. Here we were, a very ordinary group of Kiwis living at the bottom of the earth in a land of 70 million sheep and only 3.4 million people, far removed from other nations. What difference could we possibly make in the affairs of the world?

None of us looked remotely like revolutionaries, in fact most of those gathered there that night had never even left the shores of our island nation.

'Lord,' I said as I stood to pray, 'I am willing to go to Tibet, but what about all the others here tonight? Lord, why don't they go too?'

That was the spark that brought the meeting alive, and each person began to search his own heart concerning his involvement with the mission.

Neville, a retired missionary from Papua New Guinea, spoke up. 'Eddie,' he said. 'If I had the money, I would go there tomorrow.'

'I have the money,' John interjected, 'but I'm not able to go…' John was an engineer by trade, and was the leader of our Saturday morning meetings and our Monday evening prayer gathering.

'What do you think, Nev?' I asked.

'I guess I'll have to go,' he chuckled.

'Any more excuses?' I asked, looking intently around the room.

'I don't have a passport,' said Pete, a home appliance engineer. This young man was married with three small children.

'I'll pay for your passport,' I told him, 'can you trust the Lord for the cost of your ticket?'

'I think so,' he said haltingly. I was encouraged to see that my people were getting a vision not only to pray but also to go! Except for John who provided money to send someone else, each person present had left on an overseas missionary journey within nine weeks.

'In all my life, I have never had so much money coming in,' Peter told me six weeks after that landmark meeting. 'Besides you paying for my passport, I now have enough to purchase the ticket. Now I am looking to the Lord to provide my spending money.' He wondered aloud how much he would need.

'As much as you can bring,' I told him. 'There are so many needs in Asia that I take regular 'collections' from the team to meet these needs.'

A few days later, I received a surprise phone call.

'I have some parcels for you,' said the caller from a local courier company. 'Where do you live?'

When I explained that we were 'out in the country', he asked if it would be possible for me to collect the packages from his office.

'I will be in later today,' I told him, wondering what was contained in these mysterious parcels. I arrived at the courier service and signed the receipt.

'They've come all the way from Germany,' I was told. After loading them into the car, my curiosity got the better of me and I began ripping one of the packages open. To my surprise and delight, they contained Tibetan Bibles! In my excitement, I couldn't wait to get back to Betty and share the good news with her.

'They've arrived,' I joyously blurted out.

'What has arrived?' she asked, puzzled.

'The Tibetan Bibles we ordered eighteen months ago from the Bible Society. Remember? They didn't even know whether or not there were any in print. In fact, they weren't sure there had ever been any printed. Fancy, they've arrived after all this time, and very soon I'll be there. Surely, this is confirmation that God is directing our mission to Tibet. We're not only going to pray in the land, we're going to deliver the Word there as well.'

Ours was an excited group of fourteen that gathered in the departure lounge at Auckland International Airport three weeks later for the flight to Bangkok. I went up to Pete and said, 'How did your money situation end up?' His face shone.

'It's unbelievable, Eddie' he said. 'Besides the money for my ticket, I was given an additional $1,500.00.'

'It all happened because you trusted God and stepped out in faith,' I told him. 'I have done this many times. It has become part of my life. I could never move like I do if it weren't for the miraculous provision of God.'

The twelve-hour flight from Auckland to Bangkok was just the first leg on a marathon journey to Tibet. In the Thai capital, we linked up with four Americans.

They had heard of the trip through our ministry in the United States called Asian Bible Mission. We had established that arm of our mission in 1986.

Johnny Mitchell, a long-standing friend, was my choice for director of Asian Bible Mission even before it had been named. This quiet-spoken man of many years' experience in missions work (especially to restricted countries) had helped establish the Open Doors' offices in several countries including Australia and New Zealand.

As he told me of his coming retirement, I revealed my plans to open a United States branch of Mission Outreach.

'You've got too many good years left in you to retire from God's work,' I said. 'And Mitzi (his wife) could support you in this. Would you consider helping me establish Mission Outreach in America?'

'I'll do whatever I can to help you,' he responded. We searched through the names of California non-profit corporations and discovered that a Mission Outreach was already registered.

'We'll have to use another name,' Johnny said. 'What do you think about Asian Bible Mission?' I liked it, and ABM was born.

Back to our trip… From Bangkok we flew to Canton, China. That was the only possible route into Tibet and we needed to clear customs in China before continuing. Fortunately, our Bibles were not discovered as we passed through Chinese customs in this bustling city. All the reports we had received indicated that very few Bibles were getting through at Canton. In addition to the Tibetan Bibles we were carrying, we had hundreds of Chinese Scriptures. We did not intend to deliver these until our return from Tibet, so we had to carry them with us all the way.

The next leg of the trip was by CAAC (Civil Aviation Administration of China) to Chengdu on the border of Tibet.

It was there that I applied for a permit for our group to enter the Tibet Autonomous Region.

'You must remain here for two days,' a woman official informed us on the morning of our flight.

'We haven't got the time,' I protested. 'We're supposed to go today.'

The woman was not pleased at my response. 'It is impossible for you to board the flight to Tibet without the proper permit,' she snapped. 'You will have to stay!'

The Roof of the World

My protests fell on deaf ears, so I decided that we would go anyway. It was time for tunnel vision. We would need a miracle if we were to be allowed to board the plane.

'Lord,' I prayed quietly, 'I am asking for another miracle. Please stand with us at this time.'

I didn't inform my group of the difficulties concerning our permit. Our baggage was already checked through, so I led the team to stand in line for the customs check. Legally, it should have been impossible for any of us to be permitted on the flight. Still, I never allowed problems like that to stand in my way.

I handed the group's passports, visas and boarding passes to an officer. He peered at them briefly and wordlessly handed them back to me, waving us through. I whispered a prayer of gratitude as we clambered aboard the flight.

The early-morning journey to Tibet provided us with some breathtaking views of the snow-peaked Himalayas. Deplaning was also a breathtaking experience in more ways than one. We were at an altitude of more than 12,000 feet. I looked around and found that we were completely surrounded by mountains. It was a magnificent view but the altitude made me short of breath.

Another problem was waiting for us. Since we had made no arrangements and no one was expecting us, we were left standing in the airfield by the plane, about half a mile from the terminal.

All the other passengers had been collected by a bus, taken to the terminal to go through customs, then on to their various destinations.

As we stood there helplessly, I drew in a lung-full of brisk air bringing the clean scent of snow and the fragrance of pine from the surrounding mountains. I was confused as to what we should do next, so I did what I always did in unpredictable situations. I prayed.

When I opened my eyes, I saw a military vehicle approaching. A uniformed man hopped out of the jeep and strode toward us. He explained he was a Colonel, in charge of the airport.

'Where is your permit?' he asked. His keen eyes bored into mine. I handed him a sheet of paper with all of our Chinese visas on them. He checked through the documents and shook his head. 'This is not your permit,' he said sternly.

I heaved an exaggerated sigh, and said as calmly as I could, 'They haven't given me one, sir.'

He took a deep breath and held it, then said, 'Two weeks ago, another group came here without a permit and they got nasty with me. I had to lock them up until the next aeroplane went out.'

'I don't want to cause you any trouble, sir,' I said politely, 'but I would appreciate it if you would kindly help me to get a permit so I can take my tour group to Lhasa. We have been looking forward so much to visiting your capital.'

I waited as his expression changed. He paused, then with a softer voice, said, 'I will help you. Please wait there.'

With that, he drove off toward the terminal and a short time later, a bus arrived to take us to the customs area. The Colonel was waiting for us when we arrived. He instructed us to sit down and wait, then he disappeared. The Colonel had only been gone a short time when a customs officer called us to line up our bags for inspection. I didn't want a customs check at that point.

We needed to get into Lhasa, not be thrown in prison, so I pointed out that the Colonel had told us to sit here and not to move.

There were only two planes due in that day and ours was the second. Rather than wait, the few remaining customs and immigration officials decided to leave. An hour later, the Colonel returned with a smile on his face.

'I've got your permit and booked a hotel for you in Lhasa,' he said. 'You will have a long wait, however. The bus, and your guide must come from the capital, and it is 200 kilometres away.'

I thanked him for his kindness, and we picked up our bags which had not been searched and followed the Colonel. Our passports had not been stamped, either. He commandeered an old airport bus which took us to a nearby hotel normally only used by airport staff. This military man had become an angel of God to us. He even fetched some coffee and persuaded the chef to cook us a meal.

Six hours later with our heads thudding from the altitude and lack of rest, we loaded our bags onto the bus and bade farewell to the ever-helpful colonel. 'Look for me when you return,' he said.

'I certainly will, and thank you for everything you've done for us,' I told him as I gave him a firm, friendly handshake. I boarded the bus and smiled at him through the window, praying silently, 'Lord, please touch this man with Your love and bring him to salvation.'

Aboard the bus with John, our guide, we travelled for three hours toward Lhasa. Our vehicle rumbled and creaked down the road near the river's edge with the majestic mountains as a backdrop. We passed many simple farmhouses with wisps of blue-grey smoke rising from their chimneys.

As we cruised through the beautiful countryside, John called for our attention. 'Ladies and gentlemen,' he said with pride, pointing to the right, 'I want you to see the Potala Palace – the highest palace in the world. The thirteen-storey palace stands 117 metres high and has 1,000 rooms. It was originally built around 640 AD during the reign of King Songtstan Gampo, then it was rebuilt in 1645 by the fifth Dalai Lama.'

I gazed at this wonder built at the top of the world.

'Lhasa has a population of 340,000,' he continued, 'and the name means 'Land of the gods.''

'What are all those colourful flags?' I asked our fresh-faced guide as we passed by what seemed to be thousands of flags flying from fences and houses.

'They are Buddhist prayer flags,' he explained. 'Devout Buddhists believe that as the wind blows these flags, their prayers will be carried off to the spirit realm.'

'What other sorts of things do they believe?' I asked.

'They have many festivals during the year,' he said, 'several that you may be interested in.' He cited the Festival of Driving Out Evils, the Festival of Driving Out Demons, the Festival of Pilgrimage and the Great Butter Festival. 'They also have a bathing week,' he went on. 'During the first seven days of the seventh month, rivers and streams in Lhasa are filled with whole families splashing and swimming in the 'sacred waters' as they wash off the filth that has built up over the year.

'It is believed that during that period the river water possesses special health-giving properties.'

This place certainly was, as its name suggested, 'The land of the gods.' By the time we arrived at the Lhasa Hotel on the west side of the city, we were glad to be able to shower off the long day's accumulation of grime. I lay down with my head still aching and short of breath from the high altitude's thin air. I didn't want to use the oxygen mask at the end of my bed, preferring to try and get along without it. Our guide told us only to use the oxygen mask if absolutely necessary or it would take us longer to get acclimatised.

'How are you feeling?' I asked Weston, my roommate who had begun to feel quite sick back at the airport.

'Absolutely terrible,' he responded. His eyes were open, but glazed. I offered to bring him some food, but he couldn't eat. Eventually, I went to sleep.

On waking, I noticed that Weston was looking even worse. 'Move your thumb if you're alive, brother,' I said, trying to make him smile. He weakly obliged.

Moving his thumb became our signal over the next few days that he was still alive. Each time I came into the room, I would repeat the question and thankfully, he always responded. Although he wouldn't eat, I kept giving him liquids to prevent him from dehydrating. I was concerned. We were far from any place where he could receive proper care.

Through several miraculous events, we were able to meet some Christians with whom we left the Tibetan Scriptures. They encouraged us by speaking of other clandestine Christians in the land. We enjoyed seeing the sights in Lhasa, but that wasn't the object of our visit. Wherever we went, we prayed that the wind of the Holy Spirit would sweep over this land so that these long-oppressed people could come to know the liberty of the true and living God.

'Lord, bless these forgotten people,' I prayed as I sat in a bicycle taxi moving slowly through the streets of the city. 'Release the influence of your precious Spirit and break the powers of darkness in this place to the glory of Your Holy Name.'

As I prayed, a verse from Psalm 107:14 came to me. It reads, *'He brought them out of darkness and the shadow of death, and broke away their chains.'*

Our five days in Tibet proved most unusual, enjoyable and fruitful. It was time to move on to the next leg of our journey.

'Are you going to make it Weston?' I asked as he still lay in his sick bed.

'I'll have to, brother,' he said as he weakly slid from the bed standing unsteadily to his feet.

After we had completed our preparation to leave this beautiful place, we gathered in the foyer of the hotel and shook hands with the assembled staff, thanking them for a wonderful stay. We were ready for the long drive back to the airport, but we still had some tracts in the Tibetan language and wondered what we could do with them. As we sped along passing people on their way to the fields, we took the opportunity to share the Gospel by leaning out of the window and dropping off handfuls of tracts. People ran from all directions, chasing the tracts as they fluttered in the wake of the bus.

We looked back and saw people reading them and waving at us in appreciation. The airport terminal itself appeared as dreary as when we had first arrived, but it was great to see the Colonel standing at the doorway to greet us.

'Good morning,' he cried out, his face stretched into a huge smile. He boarded the bus, anxious to learn how the visit had gone.

'It was wonderful,' I told him. 'We appreciate all the help that you gave us to make it possible,' I said, clasping his broad shoulder. 'You showed us such kindness, and we will never forget you.'

John, our guide, returned from the ticket office, a worried look on his face. He called me to the door of the bus.

'Mr Cairns, we have a problem,' he said. 'There were to have been two planes arriving here today. One is here, but the other has been cancelled. Your group is booked on the plane that is not coming.'

The Colonel was not pleased with the news, and the two disappeared into the terminal to see what could be done to resolve the situation. After ten minutes, the Colonel returned.

'It will be all right,' he said with a hint of mystery, 'I have attended to everything. Just go through quickly,' he instructed.

There was no time for a luggage search as the plane was about to depart. We hurried on board as our suitcases (still full of Chinese Bibles) were being loaded into the baggage compartment. We discovered later that the Colonel had removed fourteen people from that flight to make room for us. Our great God had protected and provided for us again! But we still had another hurdle to face.

We were headed back to China with Chinese Bibles, but with no Chinese contacts.

'We have only one night here,' I reminded my people. 'I will try to make contact with some of the folk whose addresses have been given me.'

After the Tiananmen Square massacre and the political crackdown that followed, many of the Chinese believers were too nervous to handle many Bibles at one time, knowing they could easily have been discovered.

'I have one last hope,' I told those of the team who were travelling around the city with me. 'I know of a Christian businessman. He was very good to us the last time we were here.'

I had shared the gospel with him and some of his friends over a meal. They told us they had been taught from childhood that the Communist Party was their mother and father, and would take care of them from the cradle to the grave.

'There is no need for God,' they had been told.

Tiananmen Square had changed everything. Their 'mother and father' had gunned down their friends and run them over with tanks.

'We are now orphans,' they said. 'We have no mother or father.' Their story opened my eyes to the great opportunity we have in China today. The men's hearts had been like sponges, freely receiving the Good News of Jesus and His love for them. All six of them received Christ into their lives that night. In fact, I felt that if I had been able to speak to all of China right then, the whole nation would have turned to the Lord.

I found my businessman friend, and he was delighted to see me again.

'Please come inside,' he said, welcoming us all into his home. We took our seats while he served Coca-Cola.

'We've brought Bibles,' I told him feeling he would not be happy.

'That's wonderful,' he said enthusiastically. 'Many people are asking for Bibles in China.'

'But, I have many…'

'Good, bring them in. We will use them all,' he interjected.

With the arrangements made, we returned to our hotel and waited until later that evening when we were to meet in an appointed place for the drop off. Once again, we faced what could have been another impossible situation. I have been to China many times and I've come to expect miracles at every turn.

On another occasion when I was in another Chinese city with a different team, we had delivered three-quarters of our Bibles and time was running out before we had to leave. We desperately needed to make contact with key believers inside, but somehow could not connect. Each time we went to see them to make the arrangement for the hand-over of the Scriptures, they had not turned up. We were sure that something was terribly wrong. Eventually, we found one of the contacts.

'Things are very difficult and we must be careful,' said the contact. 'It has not been safe for us to come.'

We made a further appointment and agreed that much prayer was needed if our mission was to be successful. I went back to the hotel room and knelt to pray with several of my companions.

'Lord, we want to drop this 'bread' in the midst of the hungry,' I cried. 'We love these people and You know how much they need Your Word. Please help us, Father, to make the delivery.'

I opened my Bible to First Chronicles 11 believing God would speak to me specifically for this situation through His Word. In the second verse, it says, *'Thou shalt feed my people.'* I felt as though God were speaking to me through this passage.

In the eleventh verse, it reads, *'...he lifted up his spear against three hundred slain by him at one time.'*

I realised we were in the midst of a spiritual attack, and that the devils of hell had come against us. We needed to bind and cast out the three hundred demons that had hindered our previous delivery attempts.

In the fourteenth verse, it goes on to say, *'And they set themselves in the midst of that parcel and delivered it.'*

God was speaking clearly. This passage had been written thousands of years ago, and it just happened to be my devotional reading on that day. The delivery, I was confident, would now take place. My faith had been reinforced.

In the fifteenth verse, I read, *'Now three of the thirty captains went down to the rock.'* Our rendezvous was to be at a rock behind the hotel. I had planned to send five people, but the Lord said, *'send three captains.'* I had not planned to go, but knew now that I must. I chose two others whom I considered to be able to face any unexpected difficulties, and we prepared for the mission.

'We must rearrange the packing from five bags to three,' I said explaining God's specific directive.

When this task was completed, we continued praying. I glanced at my watch, and said, 'In three minutes we must leave.'

Then, I heard loud and clear, the audible voice of God, commanding, 'Go now!' A tremendous power surged through me. I felt that I knew how Samson felt when he received his strength from the Lord to lift the gates of the Philistines to the top of the hill. Nothing, not even guns, could stop me.

'Go now!' I called to my startled companions, echoing what I had heard from the Lord. Carrying our three shoulder bags, we walked briskly to the elevator. I pressed the button but was ready to use the stairs knowing that this elevator normally kept us waiting a very long time. Almost immediately, the elevator door opened. When we arrived in the foyer, I led the group through a back door.

Outside was a narrow road where cars could not stop, and there was a large, ornamental rock – the drop-off point. Our contacts arrived in a car. The timing was perfect.

They opened the car door, and we tossed the Bibles into the seat. With a smile and a wave, our secret friends sped out of sight as quickly as they had appeared.

Once again, with an audible voice the Lord had spoken, and in accordance with His specific promises to us, the Scriptures were safely delivered.

Chapter Sixteen

Miracles in Moscow and Cold Water in Havana

I wasn't expecting Rod, the young American, to be so aggressive. He had brought a bowl of cereal and sat down next to me at the Youth With A Mission base where I was staying in Austria.

'So, where are you off to?' he asked in a sort of mock-friendly manner.

'To Vienna to get a visa for Moscow,' I told him.

A disapproving frown formed on his face. 'You arrived here after midnight last night, and you were up early this morning,' he said, in a condemning tone. 'You haven't even had time to pray, so how do you know it's the will of God for you to go to Moscow?'

'Matthew 28:19,' I said.

He looked puzzled, so I recited the text: '*Go ye, therefore, and teach all nations, baptising them in the name of the Father, and of the Son, and of the Holy Ghost.*'

'Is that all you need to go to Russia?' Rod asked pointedly.

'That's all I need,' I said with assurance.

His tone suddenly changed, and he asked brightly, 'Can I come with you?'

Betty had been with me in Europe for four months but recently had returned to New Zealand. 'Sure,' I said, 'I've been praying that I would have a companion for this journey. Get your passport and come with me,' I said to Rod.

'I'm not sure if I have enough money to go,' he remarked. Not to be put off, I replied calmly, 'We'll apply for our visas anyway, and pray for the money.'

I had just returned from Poland. A car I purchased for our sojourn in Europe had a hole in the gas tank. It had developed while Betty and I were in Poland and we couldn't find anybody to repair it because it was a western car.

'We don't dare do the job because the police will come and question us for days on what you said while you were here,' explained the sad-faced mechanic. 'It's just not worth the amount of trouble that it would cause for us.'

We had been losing a half tank of fuel a day and nothing would stop it. I laid hands on the car and asked the Lord to 'heal' it. Immediately after the prayer for healing, the leak stopped and we never lost another drop of fuel until we arrived back in Austria two weeks later.

Fortunately, we were only 200 yards from a mechanic when it began to leak again. I drove into his garage and left it there to be fixed. Betty and I thanked the Lord that we'd been able to complete our journey by His faithful protection and grace. He had also given us a little while to rest.

'Call back in four days,' the Aeroflot (Soviet Airline) agent in Vienna told Rod and me. 'Your visas should be ready by then.'

We picked up our visas four days later and made final preparations to embark on a new adventure for the Lord. This was to be Rod's first trip to a communist land.

'Eddie, I'm going to blow it at the border,' he told me on the morning of our flight to Moscow. 'I'm so scared.'

We had packed a number of Russian New Testaments in our

suitcases. After Rod's expression of fear, I realised that he wanted to avoid any real risk, so I took our bags back inside and told him to give me all of the Scriptures.

'I'll take your New Testaments as well as mine,' I said, sensing his trauma.

During the flight to Moscow, I noticed that Rod had his head bowed. At first I thought he was praying but then noticed that he was really about to crack from the nervous pressure that he was under.

I slapped him on the knee and said, 'Hallelujah, brother.'

'Be quiet,' he shot back, 'this plane might be bugged.'

I told him that even if it was, it was so noisy that any 'listeners' wouldn't be able to hear a thing. The Soviet Union was still years away from *glasnost* and *perestroika,* and the hatred of God's Word was (in 1980) most obvious when one attempted to pass through customs. Even the most pleasant official could be turned into a rabid dog if a Bible was discovered. It was ironic that they spent so much time, energy, and money, declaring that they had no belief in God. *If God is dead, why are they so worried?* I thought to myself.

'No bag gets through Moscow Airport unopened,' Al Akimoff, the head of YWAM Slavic Ministries, told me.

Here I was, not only carrying my 'cargo' but Rod's as well. During the time that we were given to fill out our customs forms, Rod disappeared.

I spotted him in the most distant line of visitors. I took a position directly in line behind him. He kept his head down, not wanting to alert the immigration or the customs officers that we were together. When he came to the customs counter he was told to empty his bag. He was being given a thorough going over, and was even made to open envelopes and read his personal letters out loud. He was turning a whiter shade of grey under the Russian officer's scrutiny, and I was next. I shuffled to my place in front of another official.

'Have you any literature?' the officer snapped in a most unfriendly manner.

'Here, check it out,' I said, lifting my bag in front of him for inspection. He lowered his eyes as if burdened by the sight before him.

'Show me your money,' he commanded. I took out my notes, and he compared them with those listed on my declaration form. I was really surprised when he matter-of-factly, without even lifting the lid on my bag, said, 'You can go.'

I pushed passed Rod who was still busily collecting his belongings that had been scattered. When Rod caught up with me in the waiting room still sweating from his ordeal, he said out of the corner of his mouth, 'I've never seen anything like that before in all of my life.'

'I feel a little weak myself,' I mumbled in response, 'But praise God, we're through!'

Our hotel in Moscow was only about 100 yards from Red Square.

'Let's go and see the body of Lenin,' I told Rod. He agreed and soon we were at the end of a long line of pilgrims who had come from all over the Soviet Union. They were waiting to file into Lenin's Mausoleum. There were Georgians with their dark complexions – oriental-looking people from Soviet Central Asia. Their children wore neat hand-me-downs with red, Pioneer bandanas. There were also several foreigners like ourselves.

'What are you doing here?' I asked an elderly gentleman in front of me.

'I was in this country when Lenin took over,' he told me, 'but I was fortunate enough to be able to escape to Finland. I thought I would like to come and see what Lenin looks like now.'

A cynical smile creased his face. As we filed past the preserved body of this man who had done so much to advance the Russian

Miracles in Moscow and Cold Water in Havana

Revolution and brought so much suffering to untold millions of people, there was not a sound to be heard. Lenin was dressed in a dark suit, laying stiffly on his back with his hands crossed across his chest.

I wondered what was going through the minds of the people who stood looking down at Lenin's corpse. This man had created a Religion of Communism. There was a Trinity – Marx, Engels and Lenin. He had created holy days. He knew that the Russian people were deeply religious, so he made icons, idols, huge pictures of himself and other Soviet leaders to be displayed and worshipped in prominent places.

I was reminded of the fact that our God had risen from the grave. He is alive and His tomb is empty! The stale spirit of death filled the mausoleum where we stood, and I couldn't leave quickly enough to suit me. It was a depressing experience except for the reminder that JESUS IS ALIVE!

'Let's go find the Moscow Baptist church, Rod,' I said as we were leaving Lenin's tomb. 'We can easily walk there from here. I don't think it is far. We need to find it before tonight, then we'll return for the service.'

The church was close by, but in the short time that it took to walk there, the glum faces of the people in the streets saddened us. It seemed to me that the revolution had become a curse to the Russian people. Atheism promised material blessings but had actually impoverished the people's spirits with corruption and fear.

When we returned to the church that evening again walking through the ebb and flow of Moscow life, I felt I was part of a secret war for souls. We found that the congregation was already seated.

'Are you from the West?' asked someone who sat down beside me.

'Yes,' I answered.

'Come with me,' he said taking hold of my jacket and directing me to a staircase which led to the 'Westerner's Box.' I had been warned that this might happen and was prepared. As he started up the stairs, I extricated myself from him, quickly losing myself in the crowd. Rod, however, continued the climb upstairs with the man.

There must have been 1,000 or more people packed inside the sanctuary. Many stood reverently in the side and centre aisles, and all the staircases were packed. I stood beside an elderly gentleman on some stairs. After a few moments, I took his hand in mine and held it firmly. It felt like an electric current was flowing through me. He must have felt it too because he gripped me with both hands. *This must be the Spirit of God showing me that this man is truly a born again believer,* I thought.

I took some of the Scriptures I had packed in my pockets, under my shirt, in my socks and tucked around my belt, and gave them to him. I began to move out from the crowd and up the stairs. The people's expressions told me they could tell I was a Westerner. I passed out New Testaments here and there. People secretively grabbed them and tucked them away.

As I was passing a New Testament to one woman, another cried out in protest, but the cry was muffled. I looked up and saw a hand – only to the wrist – covering her mouth. I looked again to be sure and there it was, a hand without an arm. It seemed to me that it must have been an angel.

With only two New Testaments left, I made my way out into the street. There were two elderly ladies leaving the building. I moved alongside them and said, 'Hallelujah.' That word is the same in every language.

'Hallelujah,' they replied sincerely, then looked at me quizzically. I handed each of them a New Testament. They grasped them in disbelief. With tears rolling down their cheeks, they stroked the pages of their precious new books. *How long have they prayed for these?* I wondered as we turned the corner together.

In those days, Bibles were worth US $400 on the black market. The average believer never could have afforded one. I gave them each a hug and quickly crossed the road. As I turned to wave goodbye, they were still staring after me. *I must seem like an angel of God to them,* I thought as I walked away.

'I would like you to see a very special, needy part of the ministry of our church,' said Nelly, the wife of Pastor Raoul. After praying eight years for an opening into this land ruled by Fidel Castro, I was finally in Havana, Cuba. The bearded revolutionary, Fidel, seized the Caribbean island in 1959 and turned it into a hard-line Marxist-Leninist state. Most of the funding for his island nation was coming from Moscow. Many thought that the church there had died – just as some of us had thought about the Soviet Union as well. We were *so* wrong, on both counts!

The Cuban believers, I discovered, were alive – even thriving in this island nation, and God allowed me to bring His Word behind the 'Sugar Cane Curtain' to encourage His precious people. I went to Pastor Raul's church to deliver some of these Bibles and learn more about his work.

'We are allowed to have services as long as they are held inside the building,' explained Pastor Raoul. 'But there is usually at least one spy in the congregation taking notes or taping my messages. You see, here in Cuba, we have what is called the Committee for the Defence of the Revolution. Each block has its own CDR and they have to report on everything that takes place within their block. The CDR is the ears and the eyes of the government.

'If they feel I have said something from the pulpit that they consider to be counter-revolutionary, I am called to the police station to explain what I meant. It is very difficult for us. We do not have official license to evangelise outside our building, and I am supposed to report on anyone who is baptised. That may result in our young people losing their opportunities for further education. They know the cost, but are still baptised in obedience to the Lord.'

Pastor Raoul's wife led the way to the rear of their church building where we found a group of elderly Cubans sitting on the verandah.

'These old folks don't have anyone to care for them,' she said, 'so we do it. There are forty of them here.'

'How are they provided for?' I asked.

'The church takes full care of them,' she said. 'They have no other support.' I was shown their rooms. They had extremely poor ventilation and were not much bigger than dog kennels. The rooms were so hot that I wondered how anyone could possibly survive in them.

'We can't even give these people cold water to drink,' she said. 'It is always hot when it comes out of the tap.'

'Don't you have a refrigerator to cool the water?' I asked.

'No,' she said. 'We can't afford anything like that.'

I inquired of Nelly whether or not a refrigerator could be purchased anywhere in Havana.

'Yes, but only in the tourist's dollar store,' she answered.

As I looked at this pathetic group of old folks, all of whom had seen and endured so much, the Lord reminded me of Mark 9:41, *'For whosoever shall give you a cup of water to drink in my name … verily I say unto you, he shall not lose his reward.'*

I realised that I could not only be the means to supply one cup of cold water, but many more. I could not turn my back on their need. I didn't have the necessary cash with which to purchase a refrigerator, but I had a credit card. There certainly was a need, and I would just have to trust the Lord to repay the cost once I got back to New Zealand.

I asked the pastor to accompany me to the tourist's dollar shop where I intended to buy a fridge for him and his people. Raoul and his wife both came along. Their eyes popped out of their heads as they saw the dazzling array of electronic goods on display. In the West, this would have been an average assortment of products, but to them – living in a land of empty shelves – it was extravagant.

'Could I have one of these?' Nelly asked, picking up a plastic bucket. I looked at the price. It was US $10. *That's highway robbery,* I thought.

'Could I have two?' she then asked. How could I refuse? She and Raoul had next to nothing. Nelly was so overwhelmed with all that was around her that she began filling her buckets with various goods – anything that caught her eye. Never had this lady with so little, seen such abundance.

'That will be enough,' I said. I was paying cash for these small items and at such exorbitant prices, I knew that I would soon run out of money. Nelly and I went to the counter to pay and just made it with the cash that I had.

'Where's Raoul?' I asked. We turned around, and found him inspecting the refrigerators.

'I have found one I think will be suitable,' he said.

It was a basic model but would serve their purpose well. The price was US $700. I paused and took a deep breath. I said, 'It will make me very happy to get this one for you.' I looked around and saw that Nelly was eying a washing machine.

It's time to move along, I thought. *I'll end up over extending my credit if we stay here any longer.* The store promised to deliver Raoul's new refrigerator that afternoon and we returned to the pastor's home for our evening meal. The church youth were having their meeting that night and they invited me to stay for it. I was impressed by the fact that this wasn't the kind of youth group that I had known. These young people spent the evening reciting the Word of God to each other.

'Where are their Bibles?' I asked the pastor.

'They don't have any. This is the way they learn the Scriptures. Only about twenty percent of the Christians here in Cuba have Bibles,' said Pastor Raoul.

'What is your most pressing need?' I asked him.

'We need a million Bibles,' he said.

'But,' I pointed out, 'you only have ten million people. That would be a tithe of the whole nation.'

He smiled and said, 'There is revival in our land, and thousands are coming to Christ each month. Our church is secretly training 200 pastors to help meet the demands of the present growth rate.'

During my stay in Cuba, I met with leaders from the Baptist and Pentecostal churches. They expressed exactly the same need – one-million Bibles.

I was sad when it was time to leave this beautiful island. The Cuban believers were warmhearted, so it was with mixed feelings that I boarded the Russian-made Cubana jet back to Toronto, Canada. As usual, I had requested an aisle seat so that I could use the extra bit of space to spread my bulky frame. I strapped myself in and allowed my eyelids to close, awaiting takeoff. Suddenly, I was wakened by a shrill voice. It was a woman seated directly in front of me.

'I'm not sitting by that cat!' she screamed, pointing to a tiny Siamese kitten that a nearby elderly woman had in her purse. I looked at the screaming woman covered in gaudy jewellery. *She sounds like a bell in a Buddhist temple*, I thought mischievously as she waved her arms frantically.

The agitated Cuban hostess was losing control. 'Please sit down,' she insisted.

'I won't!' shouted the bejewelled lady, still standing in the aisle. 'I'm allergic to cats. I'll be covered in blotches before I get to Canada,' she continued complaining.

Oh no, Lord, surely I won't have to give up my aisle seat. I thought. *If I do, I'll be stuck up against the bulkhead in the middle with little room. My nose will almost be touching the wall!*

I reluctantly offered my seat to the complaining lady. I stood to let the woman take my seat.

'Thank you,' she said, pushing me aside. Soon we were airborne, and I prayed, 'Lord, please don't let all of this be for nothing. Help me to be a witness of your love to someone on this flight.'

After introducing myself, I began conversations with my two travelling companions who were both Canadians. I turned to the older lady on my right, and said while stroking her cat, 'Bella, how old are you?'

'Seventy-four,' she answered.

'Do you know Jesus Christ as your Saviour?' I asked.

'No, I don't,' she said.

'Bella, you're almost ready to die and you don't know the Saviour? Why should a dear lady like you perish and go to hell when God's love is so ready to bring you salvation?'

She was shocked at my directness, but still listened as I shared the way of salvation with her for the next thirty minutes. I turned to Samantha, the young girl to my left who had been listening in on my conversation with Bella. 'Samantha, what have you been doing in Cuba?' I asked.

'I have been with a ballet company in Havana for six months,' she said, 'and I'm going home to be with my mum. My parents are divorced and I have problems with my father.' I could identify with her on that!

I asked her, 'Have you ever received Jesus as your Saviour?'

With tears in her eyes, she said, 'I have always loved the stories about Jesus, but have never been involved with a church.'

I spoke with her a little more, then leaned back toward Bella, 'Are you ready to receive the Saviour into your life my dear?'

'I understand what you're saying, and I really think that I should,' she said, 'but I don't know what to do.'

'I will be glad to pray with you Bella,' I said. 'Why don't you repeat after me what I call the sinner's prayer.' With that, she bowed her head and we prayed:

'Dear Lord Jesus, I acknowledge before You that I am a sinner, lost, and on my way to hell. You are sinless and holy, and have given Your life as the perfect sacrifice for my salvation. I lay my burden of sin under Your precious blood and ask Your forgiveness. I repent before You. Thank You for Your forgiveness. I ask for Your gift of eternal life through Jesus Christ our Lord. I receive You as my Saviour and Lord. Please help me to live my life according to Your will, being taught by Your Holy Spirit to glorify Your holy name. AMEN!'

Bella was sincerely repentant of her sin, and wholly accepting of Jesus' sacrifice. After repeating every word, her face was radiant.

'You have become a born-again believer,' I told her. 'Christ is your Saviour and Lord. When He calls you to your final home, you will go to be in heaven with Him forever.'

I returned my attention to Samantha.

'Would you like to pray that prayer also?' I asked. Tears welled up in her eyes. 'I sure would,' she said. Soon, she too knew what it was to have her sins completely washed away. With that, I bowed my head and thanked God that I 'had to' switch seats, giving me the opportunity to help lead these two precious people into the Kingdom. Sacrificing my seat was insignificant compared to the blessing that it had become.

Giving up a few hours of personal comfort had meant the difference between life and death for my two new sisters in Christ… and their faces showed it!

Chapter Seventeen

To Catch the Wind

'Do you remember what day it is today, dear?' Betty asked over a breakfast of cereal and toast in our Tauranga home.

'Surprise me, honey,' I said scratching my head and feigning a bad memory. 'What day is it?' Then, with a laugh, I recovered from my amnesia. 'Of course,' I chuckled, full of early-morning humour, 'I remember, it's our thirty-fifth wedding anniversary.'

'This time, you're home!' interjected Betty, breaking into a wide smile that drew attention to her lively blue eyes.

'Remember, ten years ago, you were on Project Pearl for our Silver Wedding anniversary and you just made it to the phone to talk to me before midnight? A lot has happened since then, hasn't it?'

My eyes became glazed with nostalgia as I gazed out of the window at the fields that were quiet, fresh and verdant.

'I can still hardly believe that I was part of that great operation,' I said. 'Remember the vision the Lord gave me in the South Island when I 'saw' a mountain with a plastic cover over it? The Lord let me look down through an opening in the top. I could see that it was filled with bread. I knew the parable spoke of God's Word.'

This had taken place while I travelled the Kaikoura Coast. I had felt compelled to stop my car and pull to the side of the road. It came to a halt in a cloud of dust, then I heard the voice of God saying. 'What do you do with a mountain?'

'Cast it into the sea, Lord,' was my instant reply.

'What sea?' the Lord had asked.

'The sea of China's need,' I responded.

I knew the request had come from China for a million Bibles and the Lord was showing me that He already had them. All we needed to do was to get them there.

Betty cut into my reverie at that point. 'The mountain of bread was literally cast into the sea off the coast of China.'

'Yes,' I said, 'but also, it was picked up again and moved into the 'sea' of China's need for His precious people.'

'It was a mountain twice removed!' Betty added, her eyes glistening with joy, her voice reflecting deeply-felt emotion. She poured me a refreshing cup of coffee and said, 'Do you realise the hundreds of thousands of miles we've travelled since we started the mission in 1975?'

I smiled inwardly as I remembered our nomadic existence. I reminded Betty that the first gift we ever received for Mission Outreach came from my own dear mother.

'It was only $2.00, but it meant so much to me,' I recalled. 'She was the first person to say through her actions that she believed in what we were doing. Over many years, we have gathered millions of dollars for the Lord's work. Personally He has provided for our every need. 'Sometimes,' I went on, 'it has been through unexpected gifts, other times through my farm, the butcher's shop, or even when I worked as funeral director.'

She smiled as she recalled that it wasn't our own church that first commissioned us, but a small Māori group at Manoeka close to home.

'Weren't they precious people?' I observed. 'We led so many of those young Māori people to the Lord and they grew spiritually until they were the ones laying hands on us and sending us to the uttermost parts of the earth.'

Betty remembered thirteen Māori who had come with us to China and eight other countries. 'Remember when you laid hands on Lou Heni when he was planning to come with us on a trip? He died only a few weeks later' she said. 'The Māori people were so disappointed, but you said to them, 'Lou has already 'seen' China. He passed it on the way up."

We decided to call the Māori group, 'The Lou Heni Memorial Team.' They needed $48,000.00 for the tickets and in a short time, they had raised all the necessary finances.

'Wasn't it lovely to see how they were accepted by the Chinese and Asian people?' I declared. China was always an exciting country to visit.

'How many do you think we've taken to Asia over the years?' Betty asked.

'I couldn't begin to give you a figure,' I responded. 'It must run into hundreds. Getting people involved in a personal way has been one of the top priorities we've had in Mission Outreach. It's been wonderful. Every one of those travellers has blessed the ministry in one way or another.'

'Do you remember when you took Peter Rennie and Grant Allely in their wheelchairs to China?' she said.

'I can remember the sweat that covered me, but it was such a blessing to be able to take them with us,' I responded. Betty was referring to the occasion when I took these two physically handicapped men into the People's Republic of China. Peter had been stricken with polio as a child and could 'do' for himself, but he needed a wheelchair for moving around the streets.

'Grantie' on the other hand, suffered from Cerebral Palsy and needed full care. In China, he and I went on a Bible delivery together. I'd filled two shoulder bags, put one on his knee and tied the other to a handle on his wheelchair. Our contact hadn't arrived, so I got into a line going into a bank in the hotel shopping mall while keeping my eye on him. He was parked outside the door at our pre-arranged meeting place. I could see 'Grantie' getting agitated, so much so that he nearly upended himself from the wheelchair. I knew something was wrong and went to investigate. It was then I spotted a uniformed policeman striding toward us.

As the officer arrived at the wheelchair, I thought quickly and asked the man if I could take his picture with my friend. Beaming with pleasure, he took hold of the handles and without noticing the package hanging from one of them, he posed for the picture.

Poor 'Grantie' was convinced he was going to be put behind bars. He was more than a little shaken by the time the officer left, giving us a warm, parting wave.

'Our two contacts eventually arrived and 'Grantie' was thrilled to meet those believers,' I said.

'Wasn't it good that he could go on that trip?' Betty said. 'You had promised him ten years before that one day you'd take him to China.'

'Yes, I'd always told him that since he was locked up in his own body, just so the suffering church was imprisoned,' I declared.

I marvelled at how these handicapped men had desired to become part of a Bible delivery team so much, and yet many able-bodied people never had a vision to become personally involved. I told Betty that I saw our Mission Outreach teams as God's Commandos.

'We go into a country and strap dynamite (God's Word) to the target areas' I said. 'We leave and let them ignite. Later, we return to see what impact it has made and ascertain if we need to make more strikes!'

Betty nodded. 'I guess the target is the people held captive by atheism and the ammunition is the Bible,' she said, her eyes bright.

I cut in. 'Yes, honey,' I said, 'and I believe we are hitting the target. There is so much money being spent today, but nobody seems to identify the target or strap the bombs to that target. Money that has been given by the saints is just flowing away. It's vital that we first identify the target – then hit it! Accurate research is the key.'

The phone interrupted our reminiscing. It was Joseph Lee calling from Manila.

'Brother Eddie,' he said in his soft Filipino accent, 'we are moving 16,300 Bibles into a restricted country and we need a great deal of prayer. We also need another $5,000 to complete the project.'

Joseph went on to request prayer for a brother working on this delivery who was sick with malaria.

'I'll let the prayer group know about this,' I promised him. 'Let's trust God. He is able!'

My involvement with this dear Chinese Filipino began in the late seventies. Joseph Lee had been the researcher for Open Doors in the early days of their work in China, Indo-China and other strategic Asian countries. (His story is featured in Brother David's book, 'God's Smuggler to China'.)

Joseph had made many trips inside China and had played a key role in opening up the house church movement to the world. He later helped plan Project Pearl. We had become colleagues on board the Michael for that exciting delivery in June 1981. Soon after Project Pearl, Open Doors made the decision to concentrate most of its efforts in Asia on China and had withdrawn from the rest of the region. Joseph had been instrumental in establishing the Bible delivery work there, and he felt he could not turn his back on those dear believers. This resulted in his launching 'Tribes and Nations Outreach' based in Manila. Most of his staff had worked with him previously and were experts in the region.

Their target countries became Burma, Thailand, Laos, Cambodia, Vietnam, China, India and the Philippines. My vision was in the same area and it brought us into close cooperation. Although Joseph was Chinese, and I a Kiwi, we developed a mutual respect for one another and together were able to compliment and encourage each other in the Lord's work.

'Joseph sends his love and thanks you for being on the medical team to Mindanao,' I told Betty as I replaced the receiver. He was referring to a team that Betty had been a part of to the hill tribes' people, a remote and neglected group living in the mountains of Mindanao in the Philippines. I had been concerned about Betty being on this island because of the brutal activities of the communist National People's Army (NPA) there. At 54, she should have been past all that travelling in such debilitating heat. I couldn't do it and I wondered how she would cope.

Betty had started to prepare herself for this adventure by walking six miles a day along the winding country roads around our home. But, when she arrived in Mindanao, she discovered it wasn't quite as she expected. Many times there were steep mountain tracks to climb. We had sent money to purchase twenty-one horses for the pastors in the area.

On her return journey, an elderly pastor insisted that she must ride most of the time because of the rains and the paths being slippery. Betty's not the best horse rider and, in fact, is scared of them. She had not been on horseback since she was a child on her father's farm.

Warwick Hay, a dentist from Tauranga and a faithful supporter of Mission Outreach, asked Betty to join the medical team that he was assembling from New Zealand.

He had been on several missions to Mindanao and understood the desperate needs of the people there. Betty joined with others from the Philippines for a special mercy mission. There were doctors, dentists, nurses, evangelists and others who performed a variety of services. Each patient was prayed for and many were given the Word of God. More than 200 received the Lord on this trip. Vaccinations against tetanus, diphtheria, whooping cough, polio and measles were given to the children. The reason for the mass inoculation was that many were dying unnecessarily from one or the other of these illnesses.

Other medical teams had been in earlier and as a result, the mortality rate among the children had dropped by ninety percent. Many of the children were also suffering from scabies and the Scripture came to Betty's mind, *'Through lack of knowledge, the people perish…'* She used to think that this only applied to the spiritual, but with these tribal people, it was very much in the 'natural' as well.

'It wasn't that they were lazy. They just didn't know how to care for themselves properly – and they were terribly poor,' she explained.

On her return, Betty asked through our Mission Outreach mailing list that our supporters donate children's T-shirts. They responded in a wonderful way and we've since been able to take hundreds of them to Mindanao.

Betty moved on to another topic. 'Has TNO finished the remodeling of their building in Quezon City yet?' she asked.

'No,' I replied, 'not yet. They have decided to add another couple of offices and more sleeping quarters.'

Rick and Chris, a lovely American couple we had met and stayed with in the United States, had generously given a large gift that not only helped to purchase this two-storey headquarters, but also paid for many Bibles to be delivered to different Asian countries. These were vital projects that had been held up through lack of finance.

Rick and Chris have supported many missions over the years and have been guided by the Lord to help fund many special projects around the world.

On the subject of giving, Betty reminded me of the time we had broken our vow to always give all but a few dollars of what came in each month, to overseas projects.

'Do you remember that time we didn't give away the funds?' she said.

We had made it a practice at the end of every month to send out all of the money on hand, leaving only enough to keep our bank account open. On this occasion, we had not received a large amount and I decided to hold it over for the following month.

'The well began to dry up and we did not receive another donation,' I recalled sadly. 'It sure showed me the importance of never holding on to what should be sent out to the harvest field.'

The majority of the money was raised in Australia, New Zealand and the United States and was being given to Tribes and Nations Outreach.

Betty was thoroughly enjoying our walk down memory lane. Her face broke into a radiant smile as she said, 'One thing I've learned living with you all these years, Eddie, is you're not afraid to talk to anybody, especially if it gives you the chance to share the gospel.'

I smiled. 'Well, honey, I take my injunction from Psalm 96:2-3, where it tells us to *"…proclaim the good news of His salvation from day to day. Declare His glory among the nations, His wonders among all peoples."'*

Betty reminded me of the time we were relieving the local funeral directors who were overseas.

I had a body in the back of my pick-up when I picked up an unsuspecting hitchhiker.

'The fellow wouldn't stop talking, so I let him go for a while,' I chuckled. 'When he finally ran out of things to say, he asked me what I had in the back of the wagon. I suggested he take a look. He turned round and saw something under cover in the back. 'Don't worry, it's only a body,' I told him, a wry smile on my face. 'He won't hurt you.' He seemed to freeze and stared at me with wide, frightened eyes. I knew I now had a captive audience and for the rest of the journey, I was able to evangelise him.'

When I am driving in New Zealand on my own, I ask the Lord

for hitchhikers to pick up and engage in conversation. I have won many to the Lord while driving from one city to another.

'I believe each of us has a great mission field right under our noses,' I told my spouse. I recalled how one of these unexpected converts had excitedly phoned me three weeks later, and said he had since won five of his friends to the Lord. 'God doesn't just add, He multiplies!' I observed.

There have been many people I have talked to on aeroplanes. One of them was a red-headed Irish Catholic seated next to me. He seemed to be guarded and uncomfortable talking to a Protestant. As we flew between Sydney and Bangkok, I explained that our religious 'tags' mean nothing to the Lord.

'There's only one God the Father, one Jesus and one Holy Spirit, so how can we be enemies?' I asked him.

I shared that salvation comes by 'repentance of sin toward God and accepting the death of His Son, Jesus, as a sacrifice for our sins.'

As he silently listened, never once meeting my eyes, I continued, 'His blood was shed to take away all of our sins. It has nothing to do with our good works. It is a gift from God!'

I could see there were still some doubts lingering in his mind, so I pressed home the point with a sense of purpose.

'Jesus was God's gift to mankind. He died for everyone's sin, but as individuals, we must personally accept it for ourselves.'

I then asked my new-found friend if he would be willing to receive Jesus Christ as his personal saviour.

'Yes, I would,' he said firmly. He bowed his head and I led him in the sinner's prayer.

I'm always looking for an opportunity to share the Lord's love with people, but sometimes it happens in reverse. God arranges for me to meet some people in a most unexpected way.

One such occasion took place at the side of the road in the city of Kissimee, Florida. I was a passenger in a car driven by Jay Blevins, founder of Iron Curtain Outreach, and Peter Bannan, a Kiwi pastor. Peter was a farmer who had a burning desire to bring the gospel to his home area of Murupara in New Zealand. A few years before, he had called me to preach at some meetings in a country hall and on the first night, seven people came to the Lord – three of them being the children of Peter and his wife, Anne.

On the following night, four more were saved and other Christians began to appear. Soon they formed a local church. Peter was chosen to be the pastor and the church has continued to grow. Peter became a board member of Mission Outreach and was in America to help me establish the Asian Bible Mission.

'Hey stop, Jay,' I said as I saw a black damsel in distress at the side of the road. 'That lady has a flat tyre. Let's see if we can help her.'

Jay stopped and backed his car up to where she was parked. This small African-American lady in her thirties stood distraught with her little boy. One of her tyres was totally destroyed. She had obviously driven quite a way on it and it was in shreds.

I jumped out of the car and asked if we could assist.

'Thank you,' she said. 'I don't know how to fix this thing.' Peter opened the trunk of her car and saw that there was no spare tyre.

'You don't even have a jack,' he said. Jay volunteered his jack and we soon had the wheel off.

'Why are you doing this?' she asked, surprised that we would help her.

'Because we love Jesus,' I said. 'Do you love Him?'

'No, but I'd like to,' she said.

'Come on then,' I told her, 'let's get in our car and we'll go and find you a tyre.'

During the ten-minute ride to a service station, I shared the Lord Jesus with her. She drank in every word. We soon arrived at a gas station and Peter found a suitable tyre. He asked the mechanic if he would put it on the wheel we had brought along. I could tell by the woman's harried expression that there was something wrong.

'I'm sorry, I have no money,' she suddenly blurted out.

I looked at this poor lady and said, 'Don't worry, honey, we'll pay for it.'

On our return to Jay's car, I sat in the back seat with her, her son beside her.

'Did you understand what I told you about the Lord?' I asked her.

'Yes,' she said. 'I have known about Jesus for a long time, but I have never done anything about Him.'

'Would you like Him to become your Saviour and Lord?' I gently asked her. She nodded and with that, I led her in the Sinner's Prayer.

Betty sat enrapt as I shared this story. 'Honey,' I said, 'among all the miracles that I have seen in my life, there is none more meaningful than when a precious soul comes to Jesus Christ to receive Him as Lord and Saviour and become a new creation in Him.

'The Bible says, *"Where your treasure is, there will your heart be also."* I have learned that the more we hold on to what God has entrusted us with, the more unhappy we become. Our "treasure" becomes the end, not the means.'

I finally understood God's attitude toward wealth in 1990. I was in a town in the north of New Zealand where I was speaking in a series of meetings at a Presbyterian church. I was alone in the manse reading my Bible when I heard God speak.

'Son,' He kept saying, 'All that I have is thine… all that I have is thine… all that I have is thine.'

The Lord's voice began to fade away so I cried out, 'Lord, please don't go away. I know you're speaking to me and I need to know the secret. I don't understand what You're telling me.'

I began to realise that God was referring me to the story of the prodigal son. I turned to Luke 15, and read that when the prodigal son returned home, his elder brother was upset with the way his father had put on a party for him.

In essence, he said to his father: 'You didn't give me a fatted calf; you didn't let me bring my mates home.'

His father told him, 'Son, you are always with me and all that I have is thine.'

I turned to Betty and said, 'All of a sudden I saw the glorious truth in this. The boy had been living at home all the time his prodigal brother had been away, blowing it and wasting everything. The brother lived in the pig troughs of the world and finally realised that there was nothing there. He knew that even the servants in his father's house were better off than he was.

'So we see the principal of the abundance of the father's house. The older brother could have the fatted calf at any time and have his mates home every day if he had so wished.

'But he had never exploited the abundance of his father's house. He had failed to use what was available to him. He'd never asked for it and all of a sudden, I received the importance of this.'

I told Betty that I began by 'loosing' a car for the pastor of the church where I had been preaching. Within a few days, I phoned him and asked him if his new car had arrived yet.

'No, not yet,' he said.

'Well, hang on brother, because it's coming.'

Within minutes of putting down the receiver, he heard a knock on the door. On opening it, he was confronted by a member of his congregation.

'Pastor,' he was told, 'I have been told by the Lord to bring you this almost new car.' It was a top-of-the-line Commodore with electric windows. The man handed the pastor the papers and keys – and left.

The pastor called me immediately and said, 'Eddie, you're not going to believe this.'

'Yes, I am. What is it?' I asked.

Following this, I held up my hands to heaven and said, 'Father, in Jesus Name, I release the abundance of your house on my farm.'

I still had a bank mortgage to pay off.

'Lord,' I continued, 'I release my debt at the bank into the hands of the saints.'

Two days later while collecting a gift for the ministry from a Christian couple in my area, I was startled when the wife asked me if I knew of a farm where they could invest money.

'How much do you want to invest?' I asked Cynthia, the wife.

'$100,000,' she replied.

That's the exact amount I need, I thought. I told them my story and immediately they wrote out a check to cover my mortgage.

I was no longer in debt at the bank, but still I knew that I had expenses on the farm which was located 100 miles from our home. So again, I raised my hands in the air and said, 'Father, in the name of Jesus, I release the abundance of Your house on the farm situation.'

Shortly afterwards, I was visiting the farm and the man who was sharemilking with me said that he felt he would soon have to leave. I told him, 'Well, you just pray with me that the Lord will give me another sharemilker to take care of the farm.'

He didn't consider that was a good idea. 'Eddie, I think it would be wise for you to sell it. I haven't got the time to keep an eye on it.'

Within a short time, there was an offer which was exactly double what I had originally paid for it. Since then, neither Betty nor I have had a visible form of income, but we have had an invisible one – from God.

'God has continued to release the abundance of His house upon us,' I told Betty and her eyes sparkled. 'We've trusted Him and He has blessed us. My prayer is that many others will see the truth of this principle and take that abundance to further the Kingdom of God around the world.'

Our time of philosophising and reminiscing eventually came to an end. We hadn't realised how the time had slipped by, but with the sound of footsteps at the front door, we knew our family was arriving. It was a time to celebrate. I hadn't been at home for many of these occasions, so this was to be a special day that we could share with those dearest to us – our children and their offspring. God had blessed us with four daughters and one son. I had travelled many miles over the years, but nothing had brought me greater warmth than sitting in my home and sharing with them all our joys and disappointments.

'Happy wedding anniversary,' our children shouted in unison as they filled the lounge. 'Does it seem a long time ago that you and Mum got married?' asked Bless.

'Sometimes it seems like yesterday, honey, and yet at other times it seems as though it's never been different,' I told her. 'They've been good years, though not always easy. We've learned so much and experienced the blessing of God.'

It felt so good to have our loved ones around us.

'Let's have a sing-song around the piano,' I suggested.

Sandy took her place at the piano and we stood by her. We began to sing the beautiful worship song,

> 'We place You on the highest place,
> for You are the great high priest.
> We place You high above all else,
> and we come to You and worship at your feet.'

I looked at my family as they sang praises to the Lord, and I couldn't help thinking of the family of God all over the world – those precious people He'd allowed us to move among. During those years lives had been changed and we, along with them, have reached out and have been able in some small way to bless them and be blessed by them.

The phone rang insistently in my home in early August of 1991. I picked up the receiver. It was Ella, my sister.

'The ambulance has come to take Dad to hospital,' she said.

'How sick is he?' I asked.

'He's weak and struggling,' said Ella.

I told Ella that I'd meet her at the hospital.

As I hung up the phone, I turned to Betty and observed, 'It looks like Dad could be on his way out.'

I'd always prayed that I would be at home when he died and maybe this was going to be it! I arrived at the local hospital just minutes before my father arrived. He was taken to a ward and an oxygen mask was put over his face to help him with his breathing. As I looked at this little old man who once provoked such fear in me, I felt an overwhelming compassion and love for him. I took his hand and began talking to him about the love of Jesus.

God had spared him for nearly 88 years. A few years earlier, he accepted Jesus Christ as his personal Saviour, but he never fully understood the love, grace and mercy of God. He couldn't grasp that the blood of Christ cleansed and washed away all his sins however bad they had been.

I knew my father was apprehensive about dying, and God in His love to us both, allowed me to sit alone with him during the last four nights of his life. It was during that time I spoke with him about the value of the cross.

'When you received Christ, Dad, you were set free in mind and spirit, and your spiritual welfare is now secure with God,' I told him. 'You must hang onto that wonderful truth!'

As we sat alone, I quietly sang the old hymns I knew his mother had sung to him long ago. One of them was:

'When the trumpet of the Lord, shall sound
and time shall be no more,
When the morning breaks eternal, bright and fair…
When the saved on earth shall gather over on the other shore,
And the roll is called up yonder, I'll be there.'

As I sang to him, I saw behind the oxygen mask. Peace flooded his face.

Ella arrived to take over the morning shift and I had only left the hospital for a short time when the call came.

'He's gone to heaven,' said Ella on the phone. 'He had a look of such peace on his face when he died.'

A chapter closed in my life. Dad was safe in the arms of Jesus. God allowed me to share precious times with him. At long last, we had enjoyed a father-son relationship. My father had been able *To Catch the Wind*. It was an experience that thousands of others have also received during my years in ministry.

What about you? Have you received Christ as your Saviour and Lord and if you have, are you willing to go forward for Him wherever He takes you?

Only then will you truly be able *To Catch the Wind*.

Chapter Eighteen

A Tribute to Eddie Cairns

28 May 1935 to 2 December 2021

Eddie went to be with his beloved Lord and Saviour, Jesus, on 2 December 2021. *'He laboured for the Master, from the dawn to setting sun. He told of all His wondrous love and care. Now his journey's over, his work on earth is done. Eternally now in Jesus' love and care.'*

Greg Cairns, Eddie's son reflects:

'Don't pack your bags before I get there!' I called down the phone to Dad.

'See ya mate,' my dad responded. These were his last words to me.

My sister Glennie had sent an urgent message that we needed to get there quickly. So my wife Kirsten, my two children, Isaac and Emily, and I immediately drove from Auckland to Tauranga. Arriving at the rest home we rushed into Dad's room, and all gave him a kiss. I sat down next to his bed and took his hand, 'Thank you for waiting Dad.' Struggling, he opened his eyes, saw it was me and closed them again. Fifteen minutes later he was gone. Dad had a favourite saying when he farewelled someone: 'See you here, there or in the air.' Realising he had left this life and entered eternity, we all waved at the ceiling and called, 'See ya Dad.' It was one of life's truly precious moments.

My father was a man of the Word, he lived by the Word and his life reflected it. For him the Bible was not a history book, it was a living spiritual email from his Creator and contained everything necessary for life's journey. This, I believe, was his driving motive for getting the scriptures to as many people as he could.

In Psalm 139, David writes, *'Lord you have examined my heart and know everything about me, you know when I sit down or stand up. You know my thoughts even when I'm at home. You know everything I do.'*

In his 86 and a half years, my dad lived out the truth of this psalm, and as a result, his life had a positive and profound impact on many people.

Dad was born into a home where hard work and participation were not only expected but required. The home was not immune to vice and hardship, but it was a home that where, despite the challenges, Dad learned to care and love, especially his own siblings. Despite some hard treatment from his dad, my dad's heart remained soft. After becoming a Christian, Dad learned the importance of honouring your father and mother (Exodus 10:12).

Dad rarely talked about his life before Jesus. To him knowing Jesus was the start of what truly mattered in life. As a drunken young teenager, it was a policeman's disdainful comment to him, 'Like father, like son,' that was the catalyst for turning his life around. The last thing that Dad wanted was to be like his father. That night as he knelt by his bed and prayed, 'Lord, I don't know who you are, but I want you to be part of my life,' Dad experienced the reality of John 1:12, *'Those who received him would be given power to become the Sons of God.'*

Dad loved work. He loved the joy of getting stuck into something. After his marriage to Mum (Betty), he became a butcher, a farmer, a mower of lawns, a cleaner at a bank and post office, a funeral director and he even dug graves. Whether paid or unpaid, he loved to be busy.

For him the family was his God-given responsibility. He provided for us, encouraged us, supported us, and guided us, especially in the ways of God. Psalm 127 says, *'Children are a heritage of the Lord.'* Dad believed the most powerful way he could bless us, his children (Yvonne, Glennie, Sandy, Marlene and myself), was for him to serve God. For Dad, working hard was tantamount to serving God. He spent two decades serving as a Sunday school teacher.

He also had an unbelievable ability to connect with people. In ten minutes, he could make more friends by showing interest in people, than one could in ten hours trying to get people interested in oneself.

Dad never missed an opportunity to bless people. On one occasion while in Gisborne, he gave a lift to an intoxicated man walking in the middle of the road at 2.00 a.m., and drove him all the way back home to Tauranga, where he gave the man a bed for the night. It was only the next morning Dad found out the man actually lived in Gisborne and was only a stone's throw from his own house when Dad had picked him up. So Dad got in his car and drove the man four hours back to Gisborne!

'Thrust me out,' was the cry of Dad's heart. Matthew 22:38 exhorts us to *'pray to the Lord of the harvest to send out workers into the harvest.'* Luke 9:62 warns that *'anyone who puts their hand to the plough and looks back is not fit for the Kingdom.'* These two verses harnessed together in love, activated in obedience, and empowered by the Holy Spirit, were Dad's life source of inspiration.

Many would say he was a great man of faith; I would define him as a man of obedience. He was confident that if he did what God wanted of him, then at the right time resources would be provided and there would be much fruit. Dad's responsibility was to take his mustard seed step of obedience and not be concerned about the destination.

In the seventies, during the Cold War, he went to Eastern Europe and visited countries such as Poland, Hungary, and Czechoslovakia. In the early 1980s he searched for believers in the streets of North Korea's capital city, Pyongyang. He sailed a ship up the coast of communist China and under the cover of darkness helped deliver onto a beach one million Bibles (232 tons) that would reach more than 20,000 Chinese Christians. He met the governor of Washington DC and prayed with him on a visit to the White House. He also appeared on the 700 Club TV channel in North America. But one of his favourite places was the Murupara Victory Church in the central North Island of New Zealand pastored by Peter Bannan. A church that even in his later years continued to welcome him as a speaker.

He travelled numerous times to Bangkok to attend his favourite mission conference hosted by his dearly loved brother in Christ, Sonny Largado. For those on the mission teams who joined him, it was a life-changing experience as they saw first-hand the miraculous power of the Holy Spirit at work. Dad had one goal, to get the Word to people and to bless them in any way possible.

Travelling did have its challenges though, especially when it

A Tribute to Eddie Cairns

came to eating. When Dad sat at a foreign dining table and an unfamiliar dish was placed in front of him, his prayer was, 'Lord, I'll get it down, if you keep it down.'

Then there are those special father and son moments. I well remember as a twelve-year-old when I went out with Dad in his role as an undertaker to collect a body. On our way back we picked up a hitchhiker. Hitchhikers were Dad's favourite target for sharing Jesus. I'll never forget the horror on the man's face when he asked what was in the box. Dad replied, 'A dead body.'

Anyone who talked with my father would hear of the great commission – *'go and make disciples of all nations.'*

'You've got to obey God's Word,' he'd tell them. Obedience to the Word was the hallmark of both Dad and Mum's life. No matter what they undertook, in every situation in life, they would come to God in prayer and turn to the scriptures for confirmation.

For years there was a steady flow of traffic through Mum and Dad's home as people came for prayer, encouragement, prophetic words, and advice on life in general. Their home was a place of God's presence, peace, and a good cup of tea.

On occasions, Dad steadied a church by providing practical help and advice to struggling Christian leaders. As he sought God's wisdom on a matter, his advice often ran counter to conventional thinking, but he chose to obey God, rather than please man.

Several strokes redefined Dad's life and his walk with the Lord. Dad was profoundly frustrated that he could no longer be in the field, where he always thought he would 'die with boots on.'

I spent a year at home with Dad, to help with his care and watched as he wrestled with what he could not 'do' anymore. This period brought him into a new understanding, in that it was not what he did that counted, but who he was. Dad spent the next years becoming the most patient, gracious and precious soul I know. He was gentle but immovable, slow in body but sharp in Spirit, always encouraging and always desiring to serve the Lord and people. I will be forever grateful that my photo, along with many others, made it into his photo prayer book.

Dad's desire was always to hear from his Saviour, the words of Matthew 25:23, *'well done my good and faithful servant.'* Oh, to receive the crown of righteousness given to all those who love His name (2 Timothy 4:8). But to the very end Dad's prayer always was, 'Lord bring the increase.'

Dad fell in love with Jesus the day he met Him. He loved and adored the beautiful wife that God had blessed him with, and who served him faithfully for 66 years. Dad credited her as the reason he was able to do what God called him to do. Dad loved and valued us his children, grandchildren and great-grandchildren. Those who knew our Dad, will miss his unconditional love and encouragement.

Epilogue

Eddie's Legacy Continues...

In 1975, when Eddie Cairns – a butcher with no practical experience in mission, just a great heart for the lost, and in particular the suffering church – stepped out to form Mission Outreach he had limited funds. It seemed an impossible dream. But as we see from the previous pages, Eddie along with his faithful wife Betty, and the many others who joined him, had 'caught the wind'. To them nothing was impossible.

Shortly after publishing the first edition of this book, Eddie suffered two strokes, the first in 1991 and the second in 1997. Although debilitating and frustrating, they did not hinder his enthusiasm, nor did they hold him back from going. Over the years, Eddie along with a team regularly attended mission conferences in Bangkok hosted by one his closest friends and colleague, Filipino born Sonny Largado. The teams would then travel out to different Asian countries such as Vietnam, Tibet, Laos, China, Cambodia, Burma (Myanmar) and Nepal, to name a few.

Eddie first met Sonny at the Project Pearl evaluation meeting in Manila, 1982. Sonny was then a young man in his mid-twenties. A few years later in 1985, when Sonny visited New Zealand in his capacity as Assistant Program Director for Open Doors Asia, he stayed with Eddie and Betty. He and Eddie then travelled through the North Island of New Zealand raising funds to purchase Bibles for persecuted believers in China. In 1985 to 1986 Mission

Outreach raised funds that enabled Open Doors Asia to deliver 10,000 Vietnamese Bibles into both North and South Vietnam.

A friendship was cemented between Eddie and Sonny that would last a lifetime. Sonny sums up Eddie as a man who was both prophetic and a visionary. 'I saw in him a passion for God, a compassion for people and a burden for the lost. He was a real evangelist and an encourager, always ready to help anyone in need. Grace and generosity just flowed out of him.' Most importantly Sonny recognised Eddie as a man of faith and prayer.

Prayer was also always an essential part of Mission Outreach. Eddie viewed it as the 'powerhouse' of the mission. As the mission expanded into new areas of Asia and they took on fresh challenges in giving, the Holy Spirit's inspiration and instruction in prayer was essential.

It was in the prayer room in the late eighties that Neil Mossop, the current director of Mission Outreach, caught the heart of the mission. Thirty-two-year-old Neil, a beekeeper with a young family, had never ventured out of New Zealand. Life radically changed for him in early 1988 when he had a dramatic encounter with the Holy Spirit. At the time Neil and his wife Wendy attended a church that didn't believe in the baptism of the Holy Spirit and considered anyone who spoke in tongues to be of the devil.

Neil and Wendy had opened their home to the leaders of a church group of young people from Auckland who needed accommodation. One night as the group's leader Rob was preparing a sermon, he felt God telling him to go and pray for Neil to receive the Holy Spirit. In obedience he went down to the sitting room where Neil and Wendy were relaxing for the evening and offered to pray for them. Despite their surprise, they agreed.

As soon as Rob and his wife Kirsten laid hands on Neil's shoulder and started to pray, he began to shake uncontrollably and experienced complete deliverance from past bondages.

Eddie's Legacy Continues…

When it was over, Neil describes, 'An amazing peace enveloped me. I looked up at Kirsten and she looked like an angel.' Later that night he flung open the sliding doors to their bedroom, and shouted at the top of his voice, 'GOD YOU ARE REAL!' It was a major turning point in both Neil and Wendy's lives as they were flooded with waves of peace and love from the Lord and the reality of God was cemented in their hearts and minds.

A few weeks later, while they were visiting Rob and Kirsten in Auckland, Wendy said to Neil that she believed someone would drop off the team Rob was going on to Hong Kong and China to deliver bibles, and Neil would be asked to join them. One week later Neil received a phone call from Rob reporting that someone had pulled out and asked Neil to join them. Despite having three young children, a three-week old baby and a broken arm, Wendy released Neil to go, much to the horror of their parents.

That two-week trip was a life changing experience. Not only was it Neil's first time to leave New Zealand on a mission trip, but he had the thrill of clandestinely smuggling Bibles into China. It was a time of learning to pray in the Spirit, learning to listen to God and learning to obey. For Neil it was definitely a time of learning to 'catch the wind.'

The team took several train trips from Kowloon into mainland China carrying full bags of hymn books, gospel tracts and forbidden Bibles and each time the team were able to get through undetected. On the first occasion however, Neil was sure he was about to be caught. As he pushed his way through crowded Chinese bodies, a Chinese customs officer some distance away caught Neil's eye and beckoned him over.

Neil's heart sank. He pointed back to himself to make sure he was the one the officer was indicating. The officer nodded. As Neil made his way towards him, he passed the x-ray machines where items were being checked. The man spoke something to Neil in

Chinese which he didn't understand and then pointed him to the exit. Neil walked straight out, his bags unchecked, and his precious cargo safe. Who was the officer? Neil didn't know. What he did know, God had proved himself to Neil in a way he would never forget.

Later, on that same trip, Neil felt God asking them to take Bibles into the heart of the 'Red Dragon' – Beijing. Smuggling Bibles on a well-practiced route to known contacts was challenging enough. To get to Beijing the team would have to fly.

What God was asking was not only difficult but seemed impossible. The obstacles began immediately with carrying 22 grossly overweight bags filled with hundreds of Bibles, being charged for the excess weight and the bank at the airport temporarily closed all when their flight was nearly due to depart. Time was not on their side! Finally, the bank opened, they hurriedly got their money changed, and arrived at the China Airways plane within minutes of it leaving.

Miraculously the team wheeled their luggage through the 'Nothing to Declare' lane in Beijing airport without being stopped or questioned. Their troubles, however, were far from over. It was very late at night when they arrived in Beijing, and they had no accommodation organised and only one contact address for the bible delivery. They were dependent on the Chinese driver of the small minibus they had hired, but despite his very poor English and with much guidance from the team he eventually found them a hotel in a back street. As Neil explained, 'Eight foreigners arriving at a top tourist hotel with 22 extremely weighty suitcases would definitely have aroused suspicion.' A back alley hotel was perfect.

The next morning, Kevin and Neil hailed some taxis and started cramming their cases of Bibles into them. The hotel manager looked on perturbed. 'You go now? You not paid.'

'No, no,' they replied. By God's grace and guiding of the scriptures they found the address and delivered their precious cargo. The man receiving the goods then let them out of the building with a simple, 'Thank you.' It was mission accomplished. Neil had 'caught the wind' and would not be the same again.

About five weeks following his trip to China, a short stocky man whom Neil describes as being 'on fire' came to speak at the church he and Wendy had started attending. The speaker didn't have a microphone and he didn't need one as he was Eddie Cairns, who, with his big voice and passion for the Lord, was sharing about his recent trip to Vietnam. Everything he said resonated with Neil. After the meeting Neil enthusiastically shook Eddie's hand and told him, 'I've just been to China smuggling bibles.'

Eddie's eyes lit up. 'Brother, you've got to come to our prayer meeting. It's on Saturday morning and starts at 7 a.m.'

'I'll be there,' Neil promised. Little did he realise his decision to attend a prayer meeting would change the direction of his and his family's life.

His life became filled with many prayer meetings and overseas trips, which was only possible with the support of his wife Wendy who was left with four young children who they home-schooled and a business to run. Despite the challenges she never once stood in the way of God's call on Neil's life, but always released him to go.

Prayer Powerhouse
At the time Eddie and Betty were living in the country about ten kilometres south of Tauranga. When Saturday morning arrived, Neil couldn't wait to get there. Pulling up in front of a red-roofed, two-storeyed brick house, Neil followed Eddie's instructions, walked through the garage, passed a small room with a desk that served as Eddie's office and into what had been a tool shed but now served as Mission Outreach's prayer room. The room was carpeted, with couches and chairs lining the wall. A man called Skippy, a

former alcoholic who now radiated Jesus, was already seated. Over the following weeks, months, and years Neil would become well acquainted with the others who came to the prayer meeting.

Regular attendees included people like John Wright, a dairy farmer and Bible scholar who taught regularly at a local Bible College. Also Neville Pethybridge, a former missionary in Papua New Guinea and John Oram, a marine engineer who, as Neil soon discovered, had a phenomenal grasp of the mission field, and seemed to know everything about every country. And of course, there was Eddie and Betty. Later, Wendy occasionally joined them along with many others. Over the years as some moved on, others came. The room was always full of enthusiastic 'pray-ers', along with those needing prayer before going out on a mission trip, or those who had returned to share their testimony.

Prayer was focused, Spirit-led and very exciting, especially when reports came back showing how their prayers were answered: finance miraculously provided, Bibles safely delivered to Scripture-starved nations, outstanding healings and most importantly reports of new churches being established in many restricted access nations of Asia where for so long Christianity had been outlawed.

Often Eddie would share a pressing need facing the Mission Outreach Board and ask the group to pray for God's wisdom. Invariably someone would get a Scripture or receive a prophetic word that gave the Board understanding on how to proceed. As Eddie repeatedly declared, 'Prayer is Mission Outreach's power-house.' The Saturday prayer meeting started at 7 a.m. but would occasionally continue through the morning into the early afternoon.

Today, prayer is still Mission Outreach's powerhouse. Every week a group of like-minded believers gather in person or online from around New Zealand. Warren Young who is establishing a Mission Outreach branch in USA, occasionally joins from Arizona. The prayer time has changed from Saturday morning to Monday night, but in its 47 years of existence prayer still remains an integral part of Mission Outreach's focus.

Stepping Out on the Water
Stephen Woolley was another person who was drawn into the heart of Mission Outreach through prayer. Stephen, who in 1981 was living in Matamata where he operated a signwriting business, knew of Eddie by reputation only as the owner of Matamata's Three Pigs butcher shop. It wasn't until Eddie spoke at Stephen's church that they met in person. Eddie had come to share about Project Pearl (also known as Operation Pearl) and the plan to get a million Bibles into China. Stephen, who loved giving out Bibles to new believers, was so inspired by the vision that he and his wife Jenny decided to give a substantial donation towards Project Pearl. Stephen continued to follow Mission Outreach but from a distance.

It was only in 1989 when he and Jenny moved to Tauranga and Stephen began to attend the Saturday morning prayer meeting at Eddie's home that he got more involved. Although he had been filled with the Holy Spirit for some years, Stephen was often overawed by the dimension of prayer he encountered.

'It scared the wits out of me,' he said. 'I'd sit in the corner of this pokey room, wondering what was going to happen next.'

Stephen recounts one occasion when they were praying for North Korea. Neil Mossop had a vision of the huge 20 metre high bronze statue of North Korea's leader Kim Jong-il that stood in the capital city of Pyongyang. He then saw the head of the statue beginning to melt.

'Watch the papers,' Eddie declared. 'In three days, Kim Jong-il will be dead.' And indeed three days later on December 17, 2011, sixty-nine year old Kim Jong-il unexpectedly died of a heart attack while on a train journey.

Stephen remembers Eddie telling him how, when he and Betty

were looking to buy their new home, he went into what was then a tool room, and saw sparks flying around the room. Eddie saw these as spiritual sparks created through prayer and decided this was the house to buy.

Stephen saw Eddie as a man who not only had an ability to bring prophetic words to people, but someone who could also inspire them into new levels of faith. This was certainly true for Stephen. 'The water only becomes hard as you step out on it.' Eddie challenged him, using the analogy of Peter stepping out of the boat and walking on water.

'You need to go Brother. Unless you step out it will never happen.'

Eddie had a saying he often repeated. 'You pray, you give and then you go.'

He well remembers his first mission trip with Mission Outreach. Some years previously he'd enrolled in a motivational course on self-improvement in which he'd been taught that in himself he could do all things. The difference he now realised was that 'Yes, he could do all things, but *only* through Christ.' In the course he'd been encouraged to write out his dreams. Stephen's dream had always been to go to the USA. As it turned out, his very first overseas trip was a mission outreach to Vietnam.

Stephen recalls standing in line wondering, 'What am I doing here?' At his feet was a carry-on bag, so full of Bibles that the zip could hardly close. Eddie had instructed him, 'Fill the bag right up.'

'Don't they have to be scanned?' Stephen asked. 'Yes,' Eddie replied.

'So, won't customs pick up the Bibles?'

'You'll be all right,' Eddie assured him. And they were. All the Bibles got through undetected. This same thing happened on every trip Stephen undertook after that, apart from one notable exception which is outlined further below.

In the years that followed, these Bible-smuggling trips became a regular part of Stephen's life. He would often be away for several weeks at least once or twice each year; a lifestyle made possible through the wonderful support of his wife Jenny, who except for two mission trips stayed behind to look after the children and take care of their signwriting business. As Mission Outreach expanded and Eddie had his first stroke in 1991, Stephen's role transitioned to being more of a companion and carer for Eddie.

In 1994, Sonny Largado was working out of Bangkok with a mission called Tribes and Nations Outreach, having left Open Doors. He invited Mission Outreach to partner with TNO in a project called Operation 300. The aim was to train 300 Vietnamese Christian leaders in a church planting program and to provide a Bible for every new convert who joined a house church. Mission Outreach's role was to supply couriers to smuggle the Bibles into Vietnam and also to teach and encourage the underground believers. Mission Outreach provided the much-needed funds for the project and most importantly undergirded it in prayer. Over the three years of the project's existence, more than a thousand Vietnamese house churches were established, and thousands of Bibles and discipleship material distributed.

It was also during these years that Stephen became more involved in the administration side of Mission Outreach. Because of his graphic skills he undertook responsibility for the monthly newsletter. Later, he became chairman and as Eddie's health deteriorated, eventually took over Eddie's role as director. As Stephen's responsibilities increased so did his faith, always under Eddie's encouraging eye. Eddie's physical body might have been failing but his spiritual vitality and faith remained as strong as ever.

Generally, an overseas mission venture was made up of six or eight people at the most. In 1995 Stephen sensed he was to believe for larger participation. 'Go for it bro,' Eddie encouraged him. Stephen's faith was rewarded. That year 22 signed up from both

New Zealand and Australia to attend Sonny Largado's mission conference in Bangkok. The participants then divided into different teams and headed for Vietnam, Cambodia, and Laos. One team ventured into Nepal.

Pioneering Nepal
Neil Mossop had originally planned to join Eddie and the team going to Vietnam.

Before leaving New Zealand, however, the Lord spoke to him. 'Go to Nepal.' Neil knew nothing about Nepal, only that it was a spiritually dark place. Such an assignment seemed impossible. He questioned that he was really hearing from God. While in the Mission Outreach prayer room one Saturday morning, the Lord gave Eddie and Stephen visions. One vision was of a huge, heavy, closed door. As he reached out to touch the door, it opened with ease before him. 'Go through. I will open the door for you,' the Lord promised. Eddie and Stephen also encouraged Neil to step out.

So, while other teams headed for Southeast Asian nations, Neil boarded a plane heading west for Nepal's capital city, Kathmandu. He was accompanied by Betty Cairns' younger brother Peter Hockly, his wife Jan and two Filipino women Kathy and Meme. When they landed at Kathmandu airport, the scene was chaotic. People were shouting and everyone was pushing and shoving. There was no order. The five of them squeezed their way through the crowd and despite serious communication problems (hardly anyone spoke English) managed to locate the domestic terminal for the Buddha Air flight they had booked to take them north to Nepal's second largest city, Pokhara. The wooden seats of the outdated plane were unpadded but did have seat belts. A flight attendant offered them lollies from a silver dish and cotton wool plugs for their ears. It was going to be a very noisy flight. One compensation was the scenery – it was spectacular.

Eddie's Legacy Continues…

The flight took them over high jagged mountain ranges and valleys filled with dense jungle. Suddenly the plane made an unexpected descent into the jungle. 'What's happening?' Neil wondered. 'Has something gone wrong?' The plane made a rough landing, bounced along a grassy runway, and came to a standstill. Neil quickly discovered that this was a temporary stop to let some Americans off at a game park. Tourists evidently came here from around the world to see tigers in the wild. The plane took off again and in a short while made another landing, this time on the concrete runway of Pokhara airport.

Neil hailed one of the small airport taxis and started piling suitcases into the trunk. 'Where you from?' the driver asked in broken Nepali English.

'New Zealand,' Neil replied. A broad grin crossed the driver's face.

'New Zealand, Edmund Hillary, Everest. I know New Zealand. Welcome.' In the following days, Neil and the others would experience many similar enthusiastic responses, as the Nepalese had a high regard for Kiwis. They were particularly impressed when they discovered Neil, like Edmund Hillary, was also a beekeeper.

Although Pokhara was Nepal's second largest city with a population of over a million and was also a popular tourist destination, the dirt gravel roads were rough and often potholed. They entered the city centre. The main street was lined with hotels and shops, some brightly painted in yellow and pink. Many shops had cloth awnings hung out over the footpath for protection. Their taxi stopped in front of the hotel where they had made an advance booking – a double-storeyed wooden building. Neil described it as adequate and tidy with the basic amenities, but a far cry from a top-class hotel in the West.

Neil and the team had come to Pokhara for one reason – to meet a man named Samuel Rai. Samuel was their solitary contact in Nepal. All Neil knew about him was that he'd attended a School of Workers (SOW) discipleship training course run by Tribes and Nations Outreach and the Filipino course leaders, Ben Baluyot and Rudy Manalac, who were good friends of Eddie and Sonny had been very impressed by him. Sonny Largado had given Neil his name.

The next morning the five met up with Samuel in the foyer of their hotel. Dressed in western clothes, his jet-black hair was a typical Nepalese basin style cut. Neil guessed him to be in his mid-twenties. Samuel stretched out his hand and gave everyone a firm hand shake.

'Welcome to Nepal. I'm Samuel Rai,' he said. 'I'm an evangelist. Come. I'll show you my church.' Samuel spoke English but with a very heavy accent, which was not easy to decipher. He walked the team up the main street, past the hotels and shops. Cars were notable by their absence but motorcycles, a major form of transport in Nepal, were in abundance. It took about half an hour for them to get to the area known as Lakeside. Pokhara is surrounded by beautiful lakes and mountains and often referred to as the 'Heaven of Nepal'. The variously sized and styled houses were dispersed among trees and hedges. Most were built of red mud brick or grey stone. Others were white plastered. Samuel finally brought them to a small and rather scruffy white plastered building.

'This is my church,' he said proudly, opening the front door to let them in. It led straight into the main meeting room. Off to the side was a small room that served as Samuel's office.

'How many members?' Neil asked.

'Twenty-five,' Samuel said. 'Four months ago, I started a mission called The Gospel for Tribes and Nations (GTN). We want to take the gospel to all of Nepal.'

It would have been easy to have dismissed his vision as a pipe-dream, but as Neil and the others heard more of his plan and later

Eddie's Legacy Continues...

learned of his background, they came to understand why God had brought them in contact with Samuel and why he truly was God's chosen man for Nepal. Samuel shared his testimony with them.

As a youth, he embraced Marxist ideals and joined the Maoist movement. He threw himself wholeheartedly into all their rebellious activities and quickly rose to a leadership role. At 18, as leader of a very large group of young communists he was involved in a particularly bloody student uprising. The Nepalese government declared him an enemy of the state and orders were given to shoot him on sight.

When he encountered bitter dissent and opposition from within his own communist party he became deeply disillusioned. Discouraged, Laxmi (Samuel's Nepali name) abandoned his revolutionary activities, turned to alcohol for comfort, and took a job at a sweet factory working for a man called Tek Bahadur. There was something about Tek that intrigued Laxmi as he exuded a peace, something Laxmi was definitely lacking.

During his revolutionary years, Laxmi had been opposed to all religions, especially Hinduism and Christianity. During one wintery December night in 1985, he was drinking alone in a Pokhara bar, when he saw Tek walking down the street and called Tek to join him. As he and his boss sat together on their bar stools, Tek revealed to Laxmi that he was a believer in Jesus. Before leaving, he gave Laxmi a small book which he stuffed in his backpack but had no intention of reading. Drugs and drink had been Laxmi's recipe for sleep. Later that night, sleep eluded him, and he tossed and turned until he finally got up and started pacing the floor in his small room. As he did, he knocked his backpack off the table and the booklet Tek had given him fell to the floor.

Laxmi picked it up and started flicking through its pages. Suddenly words jumped off the page. *'Come to me, all you who are weary and burdened, and I will give you rest'* (Matthew 11:28). A few pages on he was impacted by another Scripture. 'Peace I leave you. My peace I give you.' As the impact of these words hit, he collapsed onto his mattress then sensed God was speaking to him, but wasn't sure. 'If this really *is* you speaking to me God, reveal yourself to me,' he cried out.

Later that same night he dreamed he was being overwhelmed by six attackers. They were coming at him with knives, and he had no means of escape. Suddenly a brilliant light surrounded them. The attackers fell back, and strong arms reached out to pick Laxmi up. Looking into the face of his rescuer, Laxmi whispered, 'Who are you?'

'I am God,' the answer came back. 'You challenged me to reveal my existence. I am the God you've always denied.'

This experience was a major turnaround for Laxmi. A few weeks later, he gave his life over to Jesus, and wrote letters to his revolutionary comrades and to the Superintendent of Police announcing that he had left his former life as a Marxist revolutionist and was now a follower of Jesus. The same determined commitment he poured into spreading communist ideals, Laxmi now poured into spreading the gospel.

Symbolic of that change, Laxmi adopted a new Christian name, Samuel. He was 18 when he converted to Christianity. When Neil and the team met him, he was 31.

As Neil and the others stood with Samuel in his small, rented church building, they knew nothing of his background. All they saw was a young man with a church of 25 members and a bold vision to reach all of Nepal.

'Let's pray for you,' Neil said. As the five gathered around Samuel, the Lord gave Neil a vision of a very large tree, with big branches. It was full of fruit. He saw God take a fruit and cut it. Inside was a little flesh around the outside, with a lot of seed in the middle.

'Brother, I believe the tree speaks of believers and also of faith,'

Neil said to Samuel. 'You are a believer with great faith, and you are going to produce much fruit. The abundance of seeds in the middle means you will be very productive.'

Although Neil knew so little about him, he had no doubt Samuel was God's chosen vessel, and that God was calling Mission Outreach to support him in his call to bring the gospel to Nepal. During their remaining few days with Samuel in Pokhara, God gave Neil further confirmation. Before leaving New Zealand, Neil had a dream which he had sensed was connected to his trip to Nepal but didn't know how. In his dream he saw a white plastered church building with a thatched roof out in the country, about two thirds of the way up a hill.

During their stay in Pokhara, Samuel took the team for a long walk into the country. At one point as they turned a corner, Neil looked up the valley and saw the exact scene of his dream – a white plastered church building with a thatched roof two thirds of the way up the hill. Neil turned to Samuel. 'I believe the Lord is showing us that you and the church in Nepal are to be a light on a hill. You must not hide your light.' During their time in Pokhara, Samuel shared details of his vision to reach Nepal and the Lord confirmed this to Neil through visions and dreams.

Although the church in Nepal was still in its infancy and had only been around for 30 to 40 years, it had recently experienced revival, especially in the northern tribal areas. Despite the fact that most churches were small, and each had only a handful of members, there was an estimated 200,000 Christians in Nepal. As a young pastor, Samuel had responsibility for the oversight of 37 churches. Few of the pastors however, had much training. Samuel's plan was to run a School of Workers (SOW) Discipleship training course based on the same modular system as the Tribes and Nations course that he had attended. It would be very practical. A person couldn't progress to the next module until they had fulfilled their commitments of an earlier one. Samuel wanted to train Christian leaders, who in turn would take what they'd learned and train others. This way they would see multiplication and exponential growth. 'My problem,' he explained to Neil and the team, 'is that I don't have the teaching materials I need. I don't have Bibles and I don't have the finance to print them.'

Leaving Pokhara, Neil and the team returned to Kathmandu where they spent some significant days praying in the spiritual high places around the capital city. One place they visited was the Temple of Sheba, built to honour Sheba the goddess of life and death. The Bagmati River which means 'mouth of the tiger' flows alongside the temple and is greatly revered by Hindus.

As the team stood to pray on the bridge going across the river, they felt the Holy Spirit instruct them to pour oil into the water. The only oil they could find was green hair oil (green is biblically significant as the colour for growth).

Neil prayed, 'Lord, as people come here to worship their 33 million gods, let them experience such a spirit of confusion that they will be led to seek You the one true God.' He'd no sooner prayed than the heavens opened and it started to rain. It hadn't rained in this area for some time. Rain and flashes of lightning continued over the Temple of Sheba area for several hours after they had prayed. The team saw this as a sign that God had not only heard their prayers but was going to answer. Indeed, just nine months later, reports began coming in of thousands along the Bagmati River coming to Jesus.

When Neil reported his experiences to Eddie, he was very excited and especially stirred by Samuel Rai's vision to train pastors in Nepal and the need for Bibles and training material. 'Let's go for it and help him do it,' Eddie said. True to his word, within weeks of their return to New Zealand, he asked Wendy to help organise a three week, 14-city tour of the South Island, in which both Eddie and Neil were able to share the vision and raise much needed funds both for Nepal as well as other targeted mission projects.

Starting in Wellington, Eddie began the meetings with a strong gospel message, then Neil would share about his trip to Nepal and the needs there. The first to donate was an eight year old girl in Blenheim. Coming up to Eddie and Neil at the end of the meeting she handed them a five-cent coin. 'I want to give you my pocket money for Nepal' she said. This was the first gift received to start the ministry in Nepal and by the end of the tour, they had raised a total of $23,000. Truly great things can emerge from tiny beginnings.

A Setback has a Remarkable Turn Around
God, however, doesn't always work in the way we expect – something Stephen Woolley learned when taking Bibles into Vietnam. Small Bibles specifically designed for the Vietnamese tribal people were being regularly confiscated at the Cambodian-Vietnamese border. Stephen figured that the Bibles were less likely to be detected if they came in on a direct flight from Australia, so he started collecting packets of the tribal Bibles and bringing them back with him from his mission trips. By the time he'd collected 800 he booked a direct flight from Sydney to Saigon, confident that by taking this route he would get all 800 Bibles undetected across the border to Vietnam. He was accompanied by a team of 30 people from New Zealand and Australia.

When they went through Vietnam's customs however, every one of their 800 tribal Bibles were discovered and taken off them. Stephen was devastated and his faith sorely shaken. The Vietnamese pastor who came to collect the Bibles was also disappointed, but not as much as Stephen.

'It will be okay,' he assured Stephen. 'The custom guards usually sell them off for a dollar each. We should be able to buy them back.'

Hearing this, Stephen immediately took a collection among the team and raised $800 which he passed on to pastor. Accompanied by a Christian tour guide, the group then embarked on a tour of a restricted coastal highland tribal area. They had special entry permits but were only allowed to visit certain villages. They spent the majority of their time there praying and asking God to move in a mighty way by his Spirit.

One village they visited had a church service that was only held every three months and people would walk for hours over mountain trails to attend. The team just happened to be in the village at the time of that three-monthly service. As Stephen said, 'Only God could have arranged that.'

When they returned to Saigon, Stephen met up with the pastor to whom they had gifted the $800. 'I didn't spend the money on Bibles,' the pastor confessed to him.

Stephen was taken aback. 'What did you spend it on then?' he asked.

'We have a printing press that was ready to go, but we didn't have paper,' the pastor explained. 'I spent the $800 on paper to print picture Bibles for illiterate tribal people where you have just been with your team.'

What had seemed such a tragedy – the confiscation of their illegal Bibles – God had turned into a victory. As Stephen said, 'Only God could have orchestrated that.'

Ethnos Asia Ministries
In 1996, Sonny Largado who had been working with Tribes and Nations Outreach moved out on his own to establish a multi-mission ministry called Ethnos Asia Ministries. He invited Eddie and Stephen to be board members and founding partners. He also invited Mission Outreach's Australian leaders, German born Rudy Bruns and his wife Kay to be on the Board.

The Bruns were working in an area of Northern Thailand known

Eddie's Legacy Continues...

as the Golden Triangle, where families were so poor that to survive, parents were selling their daughters into prostitution in Bangkok. Through Ethnos Asia Ministries, Kay spearheaded an appeal and raised $22,000 to build the Golden Triangle Mission School. By day, local children were taught basic skills in reading and writing. At night the building was used as a Bible School.

Many came to the Lord and as result the whole village was transformed.

Eddie's involvement with Ethnos Asia Ministries further consolidated his relationship with Sonny. Founding and operating a mission carried greater responsibility than just working for one. Sonny leaned heavily on Eddie's experience and wisdom for advice. As Sonny says, 'Eddie and Betty were like parents to me. Eddie was my spiritual mentor, adviser, and counsellor. His spiritual gifts, wisdom and knowledge of God's Word guided me and the whole Bangkok team as well as the Ethnos Asia Ministries international board and partners.'

While in Bangkok at the annual Ethnos Asia Missions conference, Eddie was delighted to meet Brother Yun, known as the Heavenly man from the title of his book by the same name and authored by Paul Hattaway. Brother Yun had recently escaped from China and was the first person Eddie met who was on the beach of Swatow helping to collect the million bibles. Eddie was so excited and told him about his involvement in Project Pearl. Wendy, Neil's wife, was there when they met and shared it was a very emotional and exciting meeting. Brother Yun confirmed that Project Pearl was one of the key factors that contributed to the growth of China's underground Church.

On another occasion, in November 2011, Eddie and Betty joined Sonny and three Chinese co-workers on a trip to Beijing, Shanghai, Yixing and Hangzhou where they had an emotional meeting with some of the Chinese 'comrades in faith' who had participated in the Project Pearl delivery on 18 June 1981. They learned from them that the 'Pearl Bibles' were distributed to 39 of China's 58 provinces and that as a result, thousands of house churches were planted and strengthened.

Trusting God with Changes
In 2010, Stephen received the devastating news that he had bowel cancer and would need to go through an intensive course of chemotherapy. Although the operation was successful and Stephen was given an all clear, he sensed it was time to hand over the leadership reins of Mission Outreach. Eddie who had already suffered strokes, also decided it was time for him to step down, so both he and Betty resigned from the Mission Outreach Board.

Alvin Allan, who had been a faithful participant in the prayer room and board member, took over as Mission Outreach Director. For the next few years, he extended the work of the mission by leading teams into the Middle East, Pakistan and Afghanistan. The main emphasis of these outreaches was to pray on the land and encourage the believers.

However, prayer was something Eddie didn't pull back from. He continued to attend the weekly Mission Outreach prayer meeting and even though his deteriorating health made it more difficult, Eddie was determined to keep going on missionary trips as long as it was physically possible. His body might be giving out, but his spirit remained as strong as ever.

In 2015 Pastor Tran Mai from Vietnam invited Eddie to attend the 25th anniversary of their Ho Chi Minh City Church. By now, Eddie needed a stick to walk. To travel he would need a wheelchair. It would not be easy, but Eddie was determined to go. He'd played a significant role in the founding of the Ho Chi Minh City Church, and nothing was going to hold him back.

His Tauranga pastors, David and Linda Dishroon, agreed

to accompany Eddie. Betty's cousin Lloyd Passey and his wife Sharon generously offered to cover Eddie's costs and also go. Early September, with Eddie and the Passeys travelling business class, the five took a ten-hour flight to Vietnam via Singapore. Eddie used a wheelchair and everything went without a hitch.

The premises of the Ho Chi Minh City Church were on the fourth floor and 120 had gathered in this 'upper room' for the 25th anniversary conference. The spiritual power in the meetings was dynamic and tangible. Eddie rested in the afternoons but attended both morning and evening meetings. During the ministry time as he sat on a comfortable chair on the platform pastors would come up one by one and kneel before him. Eddie then ministered to these hungry young men and women with powerful words of prophecy and healing. As David Dishroon comments, 'It was during this ministry time that Eddie came alive. Weak as he was, you saw the spiritual strength of this man. His relationship with the Holy Spirit was on full display.'

While their trip to the conference was trouble free, the return trip was not. On the first leg of their journey, Eddie took a turn. When they landed in Singapore he was immediately taken by ambulance to hospital. David and Linda continued their flight to New Zealand. Lloyd and Sharon stayed behind in Singapore with Eddie. After several days of first-class hospital treatment, Eddie recovered enough to complete the journey. When David went to welcome them home, Eddie was still bubbling with excitement over what had happened at the conference. 'I'm ready to go back again,' he declared. But as David observed, Lloyd and Sharon were far more cautious about a return visit. During their time in Singapore Eddie's health had been so fragile, they were on constant alert the whole time. And indeed, this would prove to be Eddie's last missionary trip abroad.

Eddie and Betty had built a beautiful home in the Bethlehem

area of Tauranga City and their daughter Glennie lived with them to help with their care. By 2014 as Eddie's health further deteriorated, the upkeep of their large lawn and garden became too difficult to manage, and they all moved to a smaller house in a nearby new retirement village. As Eddie became more unsteady on his feet and Betty was having difficulty coping, Glennie's support and help was invaluable, despite struggling with her own health issues, she faithfully and joyfully served her parents. Finally, in mid-2019, the family made the difficult decision to move Eddie to the hospital area of a local rest home. Some months later Betty moved into a small apartment in the same home.

By now Eddie's mobility was limited and his short-term memory failing, his spirit remained alive as ever. While he could no longer attend the MO prayer meetings, Neil who in 2018 had taken over as Mission Outreach Director, regularly dropped by with Wendy to update Eddie on MO's activities. Eddie's eyes sparkled as he recalled the old times with them. In animated conversation he spoke in detail of past mission adventures, reeled off names of many who'd participated and quoted chapter and verse of the Scriptures he'd long since memorised. Eddie's short-term memory might be letting him down, but there was nothing wrong with his long-term memory. Sadly, his physical condition continued to deteriorate until 9.58 p.m., 2 December 2021, at the age of 86 surrounded by his family, he passed from this life and went to be with his Saviour whom he'd served so faithfully for nearly 70 years.

Because of Covid restrictions, only 50 close family and friends were able to attend the funeral service lead by David Dishroon. Eddie's son Greg gave the eulogy. His words echoed the hearts not only of the immediate family and friends who were physically present, but Eddie's many friends, mission associates and acquaintances who were able to link in online both in New Zealand and overseas.

Catching the Vision – A Legacy of Multiplication

Eddie Cairns might have departed this life, but the work of Mission Outreach continues as strongly as ever under the capable direction of Neil and Wendy Mossop and the other Trust Board members – Jesse Misa, Clive Exelby, Warren Young and Alan Taylor. Despite travel restrictions caused through the Covid pandemic during 2020 and 2021, the work overseas continued to expand and in many respects has speeded up. A need relayed to supporters online or through a smartphone could often be met within days, long before the monthly newsletter reached supporters through regular post.

In recent years, the leadership training program in Nepal has extended to embrace both youth and women's ministries. Hundreds of new churches have sprung up, thousands of pastors and leaders continue to be trained and a printing press has been established. Currently Mission Outreach is working in ten different nations some of which are Nepal, Pakistan, Uganda, China and the Philippines. Doors have opened into Iran and Afghanistan and funds for New Testaments have been sent to Ukraine, Bhutan and Cambodia for the supply and distribution of Bibles in response to our new vision for Pearl 22.

Participation in Project Pearl, June 1981, was the highlight of Eddie's life. Acutely aware of their responsibility to build on the foundations that Eddie laid, and in fitting memory of that event, the Mission Outreach Board has launched a new project called Pearl 22. Beginning in 2022 the goal is to raise funds for one million Bibles, targeted for believers in restricted access nations. These will include complete Bibles as well as New Testaments and be both printed and electronic. Humanly speaking it is a daunting undertaking, but as has been demonstrated in the pages of this book, with God as partner and the Holy Spirit as director, all things are possible *To Catch the Wind*.

If you wish to know more or to receive the Mission Outreach's monthly newsletter, order a book or give to the work of Mission Outreach New Zealand or USA, please see the contact details at the end of this book.

About the Authors

New Zealand-born Eddie Cairns was a unique man with a unique mission – to make the Bible available to people who lived in countries where the Word of God had been stifled for years.

Eddie was a Bible courier extraordinaire. Beginning in 1975, he took Bibles and led delivery teams into places like the Soviet Union and Eastern Europe, as well as China, Tibet, Vietnam, Laos, Burma, the Philippines and Cuba.

His most unusual delivery took place in June 1981 when he was part of Project Pearl, a daring and dangerous delivery of one million Bibles to China by sea.

In his earliest days, Eddie Cairns was a farmer, then a butcher and later an embalmer, but when God gave him a burden for Christians in communist and restricted countries, he began his Bible-carrying travels, often leading tours of people from New Zealand and Australia. He believed it to be important for individuals to personally deliver some of the Scriptures and see people's lives changed as they got a vision for the great needs around the world.

He was also a great believer in networking and forged close links with international ministries like ASSIST (Aid to Special Saints in Strategic Times) – he was chairman of ASSIST, New Zealand – and cooperated closely with Tribes and Nations Outreach headquartered in the Philippines.

Travelling with his wife, Betty, he spoke widely in the United

States and appeared on many radio and television shows, including the '700 Club'. Eddie Cairns also founded the Asian Bible Mission, with offices in Orange County, California. In New Zealand, he began and directed Mission Outreach Inc. as a channel for funds to buy Bibles and for Scripture translation in minority languages.

In all the years of ministry, neither Eddie nor Betty received a salary. 'God has been faithful and provided all of our needs,' explained Eddie, 'and our overhead costs have been low, enabling the money to go into the field.'

Cairns was a family man, much loved by his four daughters and one son, followed by nine grandchildren. When not globe-trotting with the Word of God, he and his family resided in Tauranga, New Zealand. Eddie went to be with his beloved Lord and Saviour, Jesus, on 2 December 2021.

About the Co-Author
Dan Wooding was an award-winning British journalist who lived in Southern California where he was the founder and International Director of ASSIST (Aid to Special Saints in Strategic Times). He was also the author of many books, including his autobiography, *Twenty-six Lead Soldiers*. He was a syndicated newspaper columnist, a commentator for the UPI Radio Network in Washington DC, and was Vice President of Promise Publishing Co. in Orange, California at the time of printing the first version of *To Catch the Wind*. Dan was promoted to Heaven on 18 March 2020, after a long battle with leukaemia. His legacy lives on at Assist News Service, where his son, Peter, is now Senior Editor.

About the Epilogue Author
June Dooney (BA, BD Post Graduate Diploma in Journalism) has written two books and helped ghost-write two others. Her first book, *Tears of Intercession*, won the Christian Booksellers book of the year

award in 1991. Recently widowed, her second book *Is Marriage for Me?* relates the story of her 30-year marriage to Godfrey.

In the 1980s June hosted a popular interview program on Radio Rhema, *The June Coxhead Variety Hour*. Still active in the church June sees prayer as her priority and loves writing. She feels very blessed and privileged to have been able to write the epilogue for this updated edition of *To Catch the Wind*.

For further information and copies of this book, contact:

Mission Outreach NZ
PO Box 506
Tauranga 3144
NEW ZEALAND
Website: www.nzmo.org
Email: info@nzmo.org

Mission Outreach USA
PO Box 10431
Glendale AZ 85318
USA
Website: www.mo-usa.org
Email: info@mo-usa.org

www.ingramcontent.com/pod-product-compliance
Lightning Source LLC
Chambersburg PA
CBHW051424290426
44109CB00016B/1428